The Problem with Denny

Dawn D. Dickerson

First paperback edition August 2023
Cover Design by Sole Ludueña from Luna Design
Photograph of Margo and Denny 1942, Family photo

Published by D2the4 LLC.

www.dawndickerson.com

ISBN 979-8-9883329-1-6 (Hardcover)

ISBN 979-8-9883329-0-9 (Paperback)

ISBN 979-8-9883329-2-3 (Ebook)

Library of Congress Number: 2023913365

For my dad.

I hope you're having a great time sailing.

Contents

Introduction

None of us want to feel alone or abandoned in life. It's the type of pain every adult wants to avoid.

Imagine, then, how it would feel to be a child when both parents show zero interest in your welfare – and you've got no place you can truly call home?

Think of the confusion when the woman you once called Mom has been married at least eight times, has many affairs, and moves on from one town to the next…leaving you behind every time?

And consider the shock when you learn that your mysterious missing Dad has an 89-page FBI file and has been on the run for seemingly serious crimes that you have no clue about.

What would you do as a 13-year-old? Where would you go? How would you survive…and what chances would you have of making it in life?

That was the world Denny Ertell faced. A young boy abandoned by his parents and who hitchhiked his way across the United States to create a new life for himself.

This is a story of Denny's coming-of-age against all odds. It's a story of hope for an unwanted child. And it's a tale of setbacks, resilience, and how adults can positively influence wayward teens and gently guide them towards a more hopeful future.

My name is Dawn Dickerson and I'm proud to share the fascinating life story of Denny – as he is my father. *The Problem With Denny* is a detailed account of a young boy's incredible journey into adulthood, from around the age of 13 until he exited the army aged 20.

It is my hope that readers, through this story, understand the impact that adults have on the lives of children. While my father's childhood was disruptive and difficult, there were bright spots. Just a small amount of adult involvement through gestures of kindness or advice helped light the path to a better life.

Ask yourself, 'what if Denny was my son, nephew, or the child next door?' How might you help a child like this? Could you make a difference?

Along his journey, Denny discovered his life was not ordinary, but he took revelations in stride and worked to overcome them. When faced with the hard decisions of life and death, he chose life.

When abandoned and rejected by his mom, he found love and support elsewhere as new people came into Denny's life to give him a helping hand.

This book is based on my extensive research via the websites newspapers.com, ancestry.com, my grandfather's FBI file, interviews with family and friends, and a series of recorded video interviews with my father that took place over several years.

Other research includes information on my grandmother, who was married 13 times, of which eight husbands are documented so far. In the family collection there are old photos with dates documenting my dad's story, as well as copies of his school report cards, transcripts, and personal letters from friends and his mother.

Given the mystery surrounding my grandfather and the fact that he was a wanted man by the FBI, I'm guessing some readers may wish to learn more about his story. So, yes, there will also be a book released about this colorful character too – with a few unsolved mysteries yet to be unraveled regarding his ultimate fate.

I can't fully explain why my grandmother Margo, Denny's absent mother, was so narcissistic. I knew her well and recognized from a young age, she was 'hell on wheels.' She was raised as an only child for a few years until her siblings came along. She was spoiled by her grandparents and a flawed individual, reprehensible as a mother.

You will notice in the upcoming chapters that Denny has a colorful vocabulary. He was a 13-year-old street kid growing up in Detroit who was hardly ever supervised. He would fight his way through this life until he was large enough and scary enough to be left alone. I, unlike my father, had a sheltered childhood, but once I was without adult supervision, I too turned into a drunken sailor with no regard for propriety.

There were some instances when my father could not recall names of people such as teachers, school staff, drivers he hitchhiked with and police officers and others. The story and characters remain true, with other names substituted to tell this story.

One of the unsung stars in my novel is San Bernardino. I love history and I love this town. What a great place to grow up. This is a love letter to my hometown. San Bernardino embraced my dad, and he reciprocated this by building a life there for over 50 years.

My hope is she can rise from the ashes of arson fires, some real and some lit and fanned by corrupt politicians. Just like the regrowth that comes after a fire, she too can recover. It will take time and care. Growing up here in 1970s and 80s was magical. It was an all-American city and still has a strong heartbeat with loyal citizens and supporters.

PART I
HEADING OUT

Chapter 1

The Basement

For as long as Denny could remember it felt like he couldn't tie his shoe without the lace breaking.

Denny longed for a 'normal' home life. He wished for a warm pair of arms to smother him in hugs and hold him till he felt loved. His parents gave him life and not much else. His mother, Margo, was self-centered. She was tall, had Hollywood looks and a libido to match. Once a man was in her sights, he was powerless to resist her charms. Margo had a gypsy soul, and her Bohemian lifestyle made it difficult to form any lasting relationship with her son.

His father, William Eugene Dulin, was only around for the first four months of his life, who was described in his FBI file as 'stocky – athletic, who had a great capacity for liquor; convincing talker; ladies' man.' Although Denny didn't know about the FBI file, or that he was a wanted man in 1940, his mom sure as shit did.

His parents married in May of 1937, in a backyard wedding. This wasn't a quickie marriage, as Denny wasn't born until August of 1938, but by December of the same year, his father was gone and by 1940, his mom was only making brief cameos in his life.

From a young age, Denny realized he was not wanted by his parents. He did feel loved by his extended family, but that only gets you so far. He grew up in Allegan, Michigan off and on for his first few years, then moved to Flint, Michigan, where his Aunt Babe and Uncle Ivan lived, then he went back to Allegan to live with his grandparents. Sometimes his mom would be there and other times she would leave him with his relatives for weeks or months at a time. Either way, he sensed he was always walking on eggshells and may overstay his welcome at any moment. In 1940, Margo ended up divorcing Denny's father and had married James Robin Ertell 'Bob' by 1942. Even then, she was still not around much and divorced him in 1949.

Bob was an asshole of the first degree, but he was the only constant in Denny's life since he was six months old. Margo wasn't around, and Denny was never really sure where she was. If he had to guess she was off screwing another man somewhere. The biggest problem Bob and Denny had was Margo. Margo would leave for months at a time and when Bob would get wind she had another man, and he would take it out on Denny. This went on for several years. Bob had lost sight of the fact that Margo and he were no longer married, divorced since 1949, but he took care of Denny in the hope that every once in a while, Margo would come back to him and show her appreciation.

All of this led to him being in a terrible mess one morning.

Bob made a big mistake the previous night. Margo called asking for money and telling lies about where she was and what she was doing. Denny happened to be home, and Bob shoved him down the basement stairs and locked him in for the night.

Denny was familiar with the basement. There was a spot down in the corner where he would spend time thinking. He reflected about the moment Bob noticed Denny was taller than him, over six feet tall by that point, and he wondered if the thought ever crossed Bob's mind that he shouldn't be such a motherfucker (in the truest sense) to him. Probably not. Denny's height and being aged 13 had him considering striking out on his own.

That night in the basement, Denny spent a lot of time thinking about how sick he was of it all. He needed to do something to get away. He had run away a couple of times before, but this time would be different. This time he wasn't coming back.

The plan he hashed out was to take the large, cast-iron frying pan from the kitchen and give Bob two quick blows with the edge of the pan on the back of the head while he sat at the table eating his breakfast. After that, Denny didn't have much of a plan, but he would figure it out as he went.

Bob sat in his chair at the table with his back to the stove. Denny was released from the basement without a word, and he was making eggs for the both of them, like he always did. Denny slid the eggs from the skillet, onto plates for Bob and himself. He would need to be quick because in a matter of ten minutes they would both be out the door and off into their own worlds for the day. Bob would go to his job in Detroit where he drove a bus and Denny would be on his way to school. Would Bob ever drive a bus again? Would it be the last time he ever took a breath? Denny would decide.

Chapter 2

Back Story

The location of the house where they lived was off 8 Mile Road in the Ferndale area of Detroit. When Denny was younger, he was constantly harassed and most days he fought his way to and from school. There were three or four bullies who would kick the shit out of him. It was always worse if it happened in the winter. Getting pummeled into a snowbank or hitting the ice on a sidewalk first thing in the morning was a hell of a way to wake up. When Denny went through his growth spurt, he put on some height and weight. He was nearly 200 pounds and taller than all of them. Because of his new stature, he figured out if he took on the largest one and beat the crap out of him, the others would leave him alone. After a couple of well-deserved ass whoopings, he didn't have any more problems with getting beat up.

Denny attended so many schools that he forgot the names of half of them, just like the men in his mother's love life. His mom was a teacher, but you would never know it by Denny's grades. Margo had gone to college to be a teacher, but due to her lifestyle, it was hard for her to stay in a position for more than a year. Moves were usually triggered by a row or perceived slight with her newest lover. She chose to work in the schools because she was able take the whole summer off and then find a different job for the new school year.

Denny's report card in fourth grade consisted of C's, D's, and an E, and yes, they gave out E's in the Michigan schools instead of F's. To be fair his D grades were D pluses, almost C's. His third-grade teacher told Denny he would never amount to anything and even put it in writing, and she was not wrong so far.

In late 1947, when Denny was going into fifth grade, his mom took him on a trip from Michigan to Southern California, via Route 66, without Bob. She drove them out in a 1941 Plymouth coupe with a 6-cylinder engine. When they were in Tulsa, Oklahoma, she was firmly told, by a truant officer to enroll her son in school, so Denny went to school for just under a week. When she pulled him out of class, they continued with their 'vacation' and headed west, which included stops in Zion, Bryce, and the Grand Canyon.

One night, in Williams, Arizona, his mom had sex with a man in the room when she thought Denny was asleep. The next morning, he asked, "What were you doing last night? Who was that man and was he hurting you? You sure were doing a lot of moaning."

"The maintenance man was helping me catch a mouse."

At some point during the trip Denny figured out that his mom was leaving Bob for real this time, and that was why they were on 'vacation.'

After leaving Williams, they drove straight through to Redlands, California and arrived sometime around midnight. Denny remembered Margo pulling into an all-night gas station and asking where Crestline was. The Redlands Santa Fe train depot, on the main road, appeared to be deserted and creepy. It had imposing Doric columns and a long colonnade that caused Denny to look for ghosts amid the columns as they drove by it that night.

Margo's brother Chuck and his wife Nancy lived in Crestline and Margo was going to stay with them for a little while there. Nancy's parents owned the Crash Inn, which was a notorious bar in Crestline. Chuck met Nancy while recovering from an injury at the U.S. Naval Convalescent Hospital at Arrowhead Springs, just north of San Bernardino.

The last person Chuck wanted to lay eyes on was Myrt, Margo, or whatever else she was calling herself. Chuck was a seasoned veteran of World War II, who served in the Pacific Theatre and had earned the rank of Lieutenant before his discharge. He had attended Notre Dame and Cornell for naval officer training and attended UC Berkeley and the Illinois College of Optometry after the navy. Although Chuck was 14 years younger than his oldest sibling, he recognized she was a flake. Having all these experiences made him adept at recognizing a ne'er do well, and he knew Myrt, as he called her, was on that spectrum.

Like Denny's Aunt Babe, Chuck had a soft spot for Denny, but having Margo around for long was not an option. Denny believed he was the 'foot in the door' his mother would use to wheedle her way into other people's lives for a day, a week, or a month if possible.

Crestline, where Chuck lived, was just 'up the hill' from San Bernardino. Denny and Margo stayed with Chuck and Nancy for about a month until his mother got a job at Chadwick Rolling Hills Private School in Long Beach. For about six months Denny went to this exclusive school. This was quite a change for him, from the freezing cold of Michigan, to now basking in sunny California. He was going to school with Maureen Reagan and Hoagy Carmichael's sons.

This should have been a dream job for his mother, but she couldn't hold it together, and within a few months, she was trying to find a new job and Denny had become a burden. She made a quick trip with him back to Bob's, dropped him off and left. It was 1948, one year before Bob and Margo's actual divorce. During this time, Margo was not around. She stayed out in California.

After finishing fifth grade in Detroit, Denny attended the Roosevelt Military Academy, in Lido, Illinois. There he had to wear a uniform and pay close attention to not getting in trouble with his peers or the staff. In five months,' time, he truly found out who his mom was. The boys kept teasing him about why he was there, where he came from, etc. Denny would hear the kids whispering when he walked by and once day this kid Jimmy, who was 12, a couple years older than him, bluntly pointed out to him, "You are here because your mom is screwing the commandant." All the kids understood this except for him, he was humiliated. It was hard enough to move around as much as he did, but something like this made it impossible for him to fit in.

The next school he went to was Fort Union Academy, in Virginia, where unbelievably, she was screwing the commandant there, too. The moving around and subterfuge was a little more bearable because he wasn't using his real name. James Ertell was his ex-stepfather's name as well as Denny's alias. He didn't know why he was going by that name, maybe it had something to do with his mother going by Myrtle Ertell and to be more respectable he had to use her last name. God forbid anyone found out she was a two-time loser. She was staying in the general area of the school, but after a few months she went out to California again and dropped Denny back at Bob's.

Chapter 3

Hitting the Road

Standing in the kitchen, Denny had a moment of clarity. The skillet weighed heavy in his hand. What would become of him if he took this path and killed Bob? What then? He would never have a chance to amount to anything and, despite everything he had been through, he was not a killer. So, he sat with Bob one last time, ate his eggs, and hatched another plan.

Denny waited for Bob to leave and resolved this was the day to finally put everything behind him. This trip needed to be different. He needed to succeed and be able to survive on his own, away from Bob and Margo. Denny hated the snow, well maybe he didn't hate it if it was far off in the distance, but it made for a rough landing if you were pushed or fell into it. Having been born in Allegan, Michigan, he knew wherever he went he wanted to be warm, so he was going to head west. His Uncle Chuck lived in California, and that seemed like a beautiful place to go.

As soon as Bob left, Denny got busy packing a suitcase. Pooling his money together he found he had a buck and a quarter. There wasn't much for him to take, he found some leftover fruitcake from Christmas, a pint of whiskey and packed some clothes, including his heavy winter coat. He made sure he brought anything near and dear to him. Walking on ice wasn't fun, so he waited until the sun had heated the sidewalks. Bob wouldn't be home 'til after 5pm, so he wasn't in a huge rush to leave. He left about the time he would normally be coming home from school.

Denny began to walk out of town. He stopped at the corner market to grab a pack of Wrigley's Spearmint gum, he threw a quarter on the counter and got back two dimes. As he picked up the change he thought, I haven't even left Detroit yet, and I have already spent a good part of my 'fortune.'

The plan was to walk 8 Mile Road, which was the main road to head west. Denny walked a little farther out of town and stuck out his thumb for a ride. Almost immediately a trucker picked him up. The driver had a big-rig and was super friendly. Denny tried not to give too much away about why he was hitchhiking. He looked like he was aged seventeen, based on his size, which is what he told the driver who introduced himself as Kenny. They joked a little bit about Denny and Kenny rhyming, which helped ease the introductory jitters.

Kenny was headed to drop off some freight to a company on the west side of Des Moines, Iowa. It didn't matter to Denny what route he traveled as long as he was heading west. The ideal path would have been to go out Route 66 but heading through

Iowa meant this trip would be more of a ramble. Since Denny wasn't worried about going to school, he was free as a bird and had plenty of time, so he would just enjoy the journey.

Kenny started talking about his family and how he lived on the outskirts of Chicago. His wife was at home with their kids, a son who was seven and a daughter who was five. Kenny had been overseas in Europe during the war, and Denny knew a lot of veterans didn't talk about their time in the service, and he didn't press him to discuss it.

Denny opened up and talked to him about his situation with Bob and what was going on. He told Kenny he was going out to live with his uncle in California, although that wasn't really the plan. Denny didn't have a clue how he was going to survive on his own, but he sure was going to try.

This was the second time Denny had been in a truck this large and he was enjoying the view. His first time in a semi was when he hitchhiked out to Albuquerque, New Mexico to his Aunt Babe and Uncle Ivan's house. That time, he visited for about a week and Babe was great. Margo was the oldest of seven children, and by far the most fucked up.

When he was at Babe's house, he was happy and loved. She was fun-loving and always up for an adventure, either going for walks or cooking something fun and new. Aunt Babe kept a lovely house. She kept it cleaner than any place he had stayed with Margo. Denny could tell she loved her kids; she had two young girls, his cousins, Kathy, five, and

Patti, four. Babe told him she wished he had been born to her instead of Margo and so did Denny.

Eating meals as a family, hanging out and talking, listening to records and the radio, and playing outside were all things he did when he was at Babe's house. This is how life should have been for him. Although Denny was sent back to Bob on 'the dog' (greyhound bus), after about a week, the time he spent with Babe was very enjoyable.

The truck skirted Lake Michigan as they headed to Iowa. His thoughts drifted to the relaxing days he spent on Gun Lake, in a rowboat with his uncles and grandpa. Denny loved watching water. He enjoyed the way water cascaded off the oars as they were lifted up out of the water but was equally captivated by how they pushed and pulled the water around once they were lowered back in the lake. Ripples were interesting and made him think how seemingly small things could become much bigger over time. Just one splash of a pebble would wrinkle water for several feet nearby. When you are on the water, there isn't much to think about because you are in the moment of feeling the breeze and sun on your face, the fresh air in your lungs, and watching movement, the dancing movement of the cattails on shore. it was hard to explain the freedom he experienced while being on the water. It was mesmerizing.

Denny must have dozed off, because the next thing he remembered was the truck was pulling in to gas up. It was around five in the morning. Denny and Kenny went in to use the restroom at the truck stop. As soon as he walked in the door, he was hit with the smell of pancakes, eggs, and strong coffee, it was wonderful. Kenny asked Denny if he was hungry, and he said yes. Denny didn't have much of a plan when it came to eating other than the fruitcake he had stashed in his bag. Kenny bought him breakfast at the truck stop and told him to get whatever he wanted. Denny ordered ham, eggs, and hash browns with a cup of coffee. Kenny finished his breakfast and wished Denny well and left.

Denny sat alone at the table for a bit figuring out what his next move would be. At least he made it to the middle of Iowa. He wanted to find someone to give him a ride, but he wanted to pick the right person. Getting a ride with Kenny had been perfect, and he just needed to keep his wits about him when he picked the next driver.

He went to the restroom again and headed out the door to Highway 6. A station wagon came into view and as he stuck his thumb out, the driver slowed to pick him up. She told him she was headed to her farm in Kansas.

Chapter 4

Cigarettes and Free Sandwiches in Kansas

As Denny stood with the door open to the 1950-something Chevy Styleline station wagon, he immediately smelled the stench of a cigarette. While neither Denny nor Bob smoked, his mother did. Margo was picky, as she only smoked ivory-tipped cigarettes. To Denny this seemed to be pretentious. His mother smoked at least a pack a day and Denny wasn't a fan of this habit. When someone smoked, he naturally assumed they had a character flaw. Sometimes this assumption was wrong, but it was an indicator to him that he should watch himself around the person until they proved otherwise.

Denny asked if he should sit in the back and the driver told him to sit up front because the back was full of stuff from her trip.

As Denny sat down, he was pleased to see the front seat was like a couch. It was really comfy. Barbara introduced herself and started asking Denny why a young man like him was hitchhiking. It was almost like she figured out how young he was, even though he stuck to his story of being 17. Denny told her the same story he told Kenny, but unlike Kenny, Barbara wanted to hear more. She asked him where he came from, not Detroit, but before that.

Denny told her about the years he lived with his grandparents. His grandpa was an optometrist, and Denny stayed with him and his new wife Hazel, from two to four years old. Some of his earliest memories were playing with puppies and sailing his toy sailboat with his grandpa, whose hobbies included raising English Setters and riding and training horses.

They talked about his time in Cass City. This is where Margo's cousin Marian lived. Marian's husband was Earl Douglas, who owned a movie theatre, soda fountain, and a mortuary. Denny had been going to Cass City since he was born, but he didn't start living with them until he was five and he stayed with them for a little over a year, while Margo was on the prowl. The Douglases had two boys who were adopted, Jack and Don. The house where the family lived had a basement which doubled as the mortuary. Two rooms downstairs were dedicated to the funeral business. A small room toward the back was where they would keep the cadavers and in front of that was the operating room, where they put the embalming fluids in the bodies and stored empty caskets. When a service was held at the house, the coffin would be placed in the parlor.

Jack and Don thought it would be funny to lock Denny in the basement when he was nearly six years old. They had convinced him, while talking to him through the door that there were dead bodies in the caskets as well as in the room where the cadavers were stored. Marian had heard a commotion and figured out what was going on and she let Denny out of the basement. Howling non-stop for ten minutes had been exhausting.

When the door opened, he ran up the basement stairs and then up another set of stairs without stopping, to the room he had been sleeping in, where he threw himself on the bed and cried. Marian came up and tried to soothe him that night, held him and rocked him back and forth, but he was inconsolable. He was so upset he didn't eat dinner that night and cried himself to sleep.

When Denny would tell this story at school, in later years, he made it more exciting and didn't talk about the crying part. Adding a cadaver in the basement and dragging out the story helped to captivate his audience. He would tell his listeners, after his eyes had adjusted to the dark, that the body started to expel gas and it sat straight up. According to the heavily edited version, he knocked down the door while he was running up the stairs.

One thing about living with the Douglases that made things wild was the bodies. Most days there were a couple of dead people lying around, which was always exciting, unless of course, you were locked in the basement.

Barbara was quiet and seemed kind of sad after Denny told the story about getting locked in the basement. She said, "You sure have been shuffled back and forth a lot in your young life." She didn't know the half of it. Denny was always being shuttled around, back, and forth between Bob's and his grandpa's, then to Flint, then back to Bob, then to Cass City, off and on, back and forth. Going to California, back to Bob's, out to Ohio, then to Virginia, then back to Bob's, his movements were like relentless waves hitting the shore of Lake Michigan.

As they were driving, Denny observed how flat Kansas was. They had stopped for gas on the outskirts of Omaha, and again in Kansas City. They were on a straight stretch of road headed to where Barbara lived. The road they were on seemed endless, field after field of dirt. He asked, "How long have you lived out here?"

"I moved out here from Omaha, when I married my husband, Paul about eight years ago. We have eighty acres where we grow and harvest corn. We don't have any kids yet, but hopefully this year we will start our family."

The place where they lived was a little off the highway in an area called Oakley. "This main road can take you all the way to Denver, and you shouldn't have any problem hitching a ride here; it's well traveled."

Denny was thankful for Barbara's company and empathy. She seemed like a pleasant lady, so he wouldn't hold the smoking against her. They had pulled up to a long driveway and she dropped him off in front of her farmhouse. After he thanked her profusely for the ride. She replied: "Please wait by the road a little bit before you head out, I will be back shortly."

When Barbara came back, she handed him a paper bag with a couple of big sandwiches cut in half along with some carrots and celery. "Here, take this, I made you some food, a couple sandwiches. Try and stay away from eating in greasy spoons if you can."

Denny thanked her again and sat on the ground and ate one of the chicken salad sandwiches, and it was delicious. The bread was homemade and super fresh. When Denny was finished, he decided he should head out while it was still light outside. Back on the highway he stuck out his thumb.

Chapter 5

No Need for this Kind of Speed!

Denny stood by the side of the road for about an hour. Not many cars were driving past. About the time he was feeling like he might not get a ride and may need to find a spot to sleep, a dark red car pulled up. The driver told him he wanted some company, and he was headed to San Francisco. The front seat was a two-tone bench seat and the driver, Ray, told him to sit up front. Denny could tell he was super excited about his car.

Ray exuberantly gushed, "This is a Chrysler, 1952, New Yorker Deluxe convertible and it came with a factory V-8 engine. I just picked this up in Detroit and I'm driving home." Although Denny didn't understand a lot about cars, he did like certain models; this car was dreamy. Ray's car was brand new; Denny had never been in a new car.

Denny encouraged Ray to talk about his car, which he did, going through all the details from the color of the car, which was a special kind of red, to the tiniest minutiae about the engine, interior, options such as power windows and convertible top, air conditioning, fog lamps, power steering, and mildly interesting features about the interior, like the sun visors. Denny was happy to listen, as this kept the focus off him. Ray also showed him how things worked or instructed Denny what knobs to turn or push to demonstrate the aspects of the car. It was funny how he got super excited about how the power windows dropped into the door so that the top of the window was not protruding.

After about an hour, Denny started to notice how fast they were going. A glimpse of the speedometer showed they were traveling at an unbelievable 100mph. The road was straight and narrow, and Ray never let the speed fall below a hundred. This scared the shit out of Denny. They would pass a car every couple of minutes, of course on the left, driving the wrong way, as they were on a two-lane road. Denny had never traveled this fast and wanted out. Yes, this was a quick way to get to California, but it was too nerve-wracking. He stayed quiet for an hour as the sun was setting. It was getting dark, and Denny was becoming increasingly uncomfortable with the speed, but it didn't faze Ray at all.

Up ahead, there was a mileage sign that showed Denver was about 60 miles away. Denny breathed a sigh of relief; finally, a place to get off this wild ride. At the same time, they passed the sign, Ray asked, "Where are you going? We never talked about that. I'm guessing you are headed west, but I'm not sure how far you're going."

"I'm going to Denver!" Denny pointed insistently ahead. "You can let me out at the city limit." Immediately he felt a sense of relief knowing this part of his trip was almost over.

As Ray pulled off the highway to find a gas station and let Denny out, they drove past a bus stop. Denny thanked Ray for the ride but what he was most thankful for was to be alive and out of that beautiful, scary car. Upon exiting the vehicle, he wanted to kiss the ground. His legs were wobbly, as if he had gone to a carnival and went on one of those spinning rides. What he needed next was some time to decompress.

He walked to the bus stop and sat down. Denny used his suitcase as a table, ate another half of a sandwich and took a couple long pulls on his pint of whiskey. As he sat there, he hoped he could find a bus that would take him around Denver. He'd never been to Colorado before. It was getting late, and Denny wanted to go someplace where it was warm.

After twenty minutes a bus showed up. Normally bus fare was around ten cents, in Denny's experience. As he stepped on the bus, the driver asked him, "Are you a student? If you are a student, you ride for free."

Denny replied, "Yes, of course, I am a student."

"Where are you headed?"

"Where does this bus go?"

"This bus drives the loop through the city and goes through Denver to Golden."

"Thanks, I'll be going to the end of the line,"

Denny found the bus empty except for one lady and the driver. He was happy his immense wealth of a dollar and 20 cents was still intact. It was warm on the bus and the ride was smooth, he was able to spread out and relax, which was a welcome respite from his last ride. From being on high alert, Denny all of sudden felt extremely tired; he must have dozed off for about 20 minutes. After he woke up, they drove on for another half hour and the route ended at Golden like the driver had told him. When he got off the bus, the driver directed him to the main highway entrance, but he failed to mention it was illegal to hitchhike in Golden, Colorado.

By now it was dark, and Denny thought he might have an issue finding a ride. He stayed near the on-ramp to the highway but did walk down to a culvert and drank a little more whiskey to warm up and ate some fruitcake. It was getting dark, so it was probably around 8pm or 9pm. Denny didn't own a watch, so he was always estimating time. As he came out of the culvert, he stuck his thumb out and had been waiting for 30 minutes with no action.

He was staring off in the distance when he heard a car come up behind him. The car shined a spotlight on him and was stopping. Denny thought, 'What the hell, is some shit about to go down?' Standing stone still, he noticed a cop had got out of the car and was standing behind the light. Denny didn't have much experience with the police, only the ones who would hassle him if played hooky from school. This was a different level and way more serious. Denny was going to play it cool.

As Denny stood there, he was aware the police officer was sizing him up. Denny left his hands down to his sides and said, "Hello sir."

"Hi, I am the night watch officer, and my name is Officer Smith. What is your name?"

"I'm Denny Ertell."

"What are you doing out here by the side of the road?"

"I am hitchhiking to California."

"Well, that's illegal in Golden and I am going to need to take you into the station. You look like you are too young to be out on your own anyway."

'Dammit!' This might derail his plan to go to California.

From the beginning of this trip, he knew he would need to go where the road took him, so this was going to be part of the adventure, but hopefully not the end. Denny got in the police car and sat quietly with his belongings next to him. They took off and as promised they wound up at the police station. The building was an old two-story structure probably built in the early 1900s. When he got out of the car, he was directed to the inside of the building, where the same officer took his information.

When they got settled inside, the questions continued but this time the cop was taking notes.

"Do you have any ID?"

Denny mumbled, "I don't know what that is."

"It's a piece of paper or card that has your birthdate, address, and other information on it to help identify you, it's your identification, we say ID for short."

"No, I don't have that."

"Where are you from?"

"Detroit, Michigan."

"How old are you?"

"Thirteen,"

"Why are you hitchhiking?"

"I am going to California to live with my uncle."

"Why are you hitching instead of taking a bus?"

"I had to leave because my stepdad was beating the crap out of me, and I did not want to fight anymore."

"Where is your mother?"

"I have no idea. She might be in California, or... anywhere really."

"Well, you are too young to be on your own, so either we send you back to Michigan or to another relative who can take care of you. How can I reach your stepdad?"

Denny gave him the number and the officer said, "Since it's nighttime, we can store your gear here and you can sleep upstairs in one of the cells. You aren't under arrest; you're only being detained until we figure out where to send you."

Denny was both frightened and relieved at the same time. At the very least he had a place to sleep for the night, because it was cold as balls outside, but he wasn't sure what would happen tomorrow. The police station smelled exactly how he thought it would. Officer Smith directed him up the stairs to where the holding cells were. There were three cells, and it looked like Denny would be sleeping in the middle one. The cop opened it up, pointed at the door and said, "I need to lock this, it's the policy."

Denny asked, "Do you have any water?"

"I'll be back with that in a bit." Sure enough, he came back with not only water, but a dinner roll, a large bowl of Rice Krispies, a spoon, and a milk carton.

"Thank you very much, you have no idea how much I appreciate this." After Denny ate, he laid back and was so exhausted he fell into a dreamless sleep...until he was jolted awake by loud shrieking.

Chapter 6

Jail and Freedom

As Denny became aware of his surroundings, he remembered he was in jail and was abruptly conscious of two additional 'prisoners.' In the cell to his left was a stinky drunk and on the other side was a woman with hardly any clothes on screaming at the drunk. Denny was in the middle of this twosome.

The woman was teasing the drunk, "Do you want some of this? Come and get some of this!" She had pulled her top off and her tits were flopping around.

The drunk was pushing up against the bars on the other side of Denny's cell and yelling and slurring, "Yas, I doooo!"

At first Denny thought they were together, but Denny quickly recognized she was a hooker. She was enjoying getting the drunk riled up.

She was yelling, "How much money you got? This isn't free!" This was a constant, antagonizing mantra. At this point she had put her blouse back on but had lifted her skirt so the drunk could see everything and was screaming at him again, the same chant. The open bars in the cells also gave Denny an unsolicited show. He thought, 'I'm a fan of the female body, but this is disgusting.' She kept thrusting her 'snatch' up against the bars on Denny's side. Denny stepped to the corner of the cell farthest away from them. Standing there, he closed his eyes and hoped they would both magically disappear.

This went on for about ten minutes and didn't end when one of the cops came up with breakfast for Denny. He yelled out the door to the staircase, "Hey, we gotta get this kid out of here!"

Lickety-split, another cop came up and let him out of the cell and he was back downstairs to a much calmer environment, enjoying his breakfast on the bench in the foyer.

Denny sat on the bench for about two hours, which was fine with him. Some phone calls were being made, and he caught his name being mentioned a couple of times. Going back to Michigan wasn't an option, and he hoped that wasn't being considered, but he was at the mercy of the Golden Police Department.

One of the cops called him over to where he was sitting and motioned for him to sit down. Denny was told they had gotten hold of Bob and he didn't want him back. Did Denny have any suggestions about where else he could go? Denny brought up his Aunt Babe and gave him her number. The cop told him to go back to the bench and he would call him in a bit. By now it was a little after 11am. He was getting antsy to be back on the road, but he wasn't going anywhere right now, so he bided his time.

Denny was people-watching and eavesdropping on various phone calls when, around noon, the same officer called him over and said, "I got hold of your Aunt Babe and we are going to put you on the Greyhound bus to her house. She will pick you up at the station in Albuquerque. Some of the officers got together and we pooled our money and came up with a little over $12 for your bus fare and you can probably grab a sandwich with anything that is left over. I'll have an officer take you to the bus station shortly."

This was much better news than he expected. Denny wanted to see how this would play out and tried not to give away how happy he was, politely thanking everyone who contributed to help him.

Denny collected his stuff and sat on the bench waiting to leave. For the second time in 24 hours, he was going to ride in a police car. An officer came over and asked him to follow him. Denny got in the backseat of the car, and they drove for about 15 minutes to the bus station.

Golden was a small town, with one main street, however Denver was larger and more sprawling. They passed a movie theatre district before they got to the bus station. When the cop stopped the car, he explained they were two blocks away from the Greyhound station and pointed out where it was. The cop explained the bus wouldn't leave for a while so he may as well find a bite to eat and then buy his ticket.

Denny went to a diner and bought a sandwich and a chocolate malt. Thinking about what his next move should be, he decided he was going to California; he would definitely be more careful. Once he got to San Bernardino, Denny would call his Aunt Babe and explain what he was doing.

To make sure he had completely ditched the cops, Denny figured he would go to a matinee movie. The theatres in Denver were amazing, but Denny wasn't examining the architecture, he wanted to pick an entertaining movie. The movie he chose was *The Texas Rangers*. Denny became engrossed in the plot as if he was in the movie with the main characters. George Montgomery, the lead, was known for being stoic and manly. The movie was engrossing and as with all movies, Denny was sad for it end. Every time he watched a movie, he wanted it to continue forever.

After the movie, he walked out to the main road in Denver, which was by the Greyhound station. Distancing himself a bit from the buses, he stuck out his thumb. Denny kept walking along the road, but he wasn't afraid of walking all the way to Golden, because it was at least ten miles away. Since it was light outside it was much easier to see who was driving past him. Hopefully, the next driver would be just as relaxed as Kenny and Barbara had been—and not some maniac like Ray. Whoever it was, he wanted to be sure they were going to Southern California. It would be great to get one ride and be off the road. He was deep in thought about his future when a green pick-up truck pulled up.

Chapter 7

Tom

Denny opened the door, and the driver asked him where he was going. Denny didn't pull any punches, telling him, "San Bernardino, California."

The driver said, "To hell you say, this is your lucky day! That's where I live." Denny did feel lucky as he got into the truck after throwing his gear in the back.

Tom, the driver, had introduced himself as Denny sat down. Denny instantly liked him. Tom told him he had a fantastic job at Kaiser Steel in Fontana, and he lived with his wife and grown kids, a girl, and a boy, on the outskirts of San Bernardino. The farm he owned consisted of five acres with chickens, cows, goats, and even a horse. Tom told him he hadn't served in the war due to respiratory issues, but he did his part working in the steel mill to supply steel to the shipyards that were building battleships during the war.

Tom asked Denny why he was hitchhiking, and Denny held back some information, like recently getting out of jail, and how old he really was. Other than that, he was open about everything else, although he did stick to his story about going to live with his uncle.

Tom was quite a character. Unlike Denny, he came from a large family who were forced to come out west due to the Dust Bowl. He had come from visiting some of his family who had relocated to Denver. The tragic stories Tom told about the dirt-wind storms and how he ended up living in California held Denny's attention while they were traveling. Before talking to Tom, Denny had never heard of how many people left Oklahoma and relocated to the west. Tom was the oldest of ten kids, eight of whom survived to adulthood. To hear him talk about all the problems he had encountered, including breathing problems from all the dust he had inhaled, and to be sitting with Tom, at this time, made Denny feel like he didn't have it so rough. As Denny contemplated this, he made a mental note to keep this thought with him always. Although life may have been bad at that moment, things could always be much worse.

Tom told Denny that they were going to stop somewhere along the route, for a quick nap, but only if he got tired. It was about 20 hours to San Bernardino, and he would more than likely need to take a break. He asked Denny if he had his driving license and Denny had to tell him no. Tom told him no big deal; he was glad for the company.

The route they took to leave Denver was beautiful and had a lot of passes that climbed over the Rockies. Tom knew a little something about everything and explained how high the Rockies were, how long they went on for, what the highest peaks were, etc. Tom said, "We will be in Utah soon. A lot of the people who live there are Mormon."

Tom took a while to explain Mormon history and how they built colonies in Salt Lake City, Utah, and San Bernardino, California. Nearly all of their members fled Illinois due to religious persecution and traveled the distance in covered wagons. Tom told him about the temples they had built; the largest one was Salt Lake City, built in the 1800s. Denny was fascinated that a group of people would migrate west for religion. It was pretty unbelievable, but he had never gone to church. If God really existed, Denny believed he or she had abandoned him, just like his parents.

Tom had some interesting views on religion, he said it kept the family together, and if his wife wanted to go to church on Sundays he would go too. Religion to him was more about being part of a group of people who helped and supported each other. The social aspect kept him coming back. They went to a Baptist church, but it didn't matter to him what religion it was. When he participated in events at church, he felt a sense of community. Tom told Denny, "You can bet if the minister gets too preachy or churchy, I will shop around for another church."

Tom was acquainted with quite a few Mormons and said they were decent people, but they did go to church a lot. It was too much of a commitment for him. Sundays only worked for him, and the occasional church picnic or rummage sale was okay.

As they swung into the Great Basin of Utah, Denny was amazed at how barren this area was. They drove in a small desert town called Thistle, Tom joked, "With a name like Thistle this town will make you bristle!" It was here Tom stopped and said was going to catch a little bit of sleep. It had to be around midnight or so. Tom pulled out a blanket from behind the seat and Denny used his coat for warmth. Denny leaned up against the locked door and shortly afterwards, they both dozed off.

Denny was startled awake when Tom started the truck. Tom drove over to the gas pumps and threw Denny two donuts and handed him a cup of coffee when he got back in the cab. He said, "Today's plan is to make it to San Bernardino. It's basically a straight shot and with any luck we'll be there before dark."

Denny started thinking hard about what was up next for him. There was no plan, and he was not sure what he was going to do once he arrived in San Bernardino. He supposed he would have Tom drop him off at his Uncle Chuck's and see if he could stay with him for a night. After that he would kick around and try to work out his living arrangement. At least he had cash and could afford to eat for a bit thanks to the Golden Police Department. This was exciting and scary at the same time.

Denny remembered his Uncle Chuck lived in the north end of San Bernardino, by a place called Little Mountain. Worse case, he would have Tom drop him off at a pay phone near that area and walk to his house.

What he desperately wanted to know was—where the fuck was his mom? Last he heard she was living at the beach and teaching school, but he wasn't sure if that was still the case. The letters he received from her talked about the beach and her 'friend' Jeanna.

She would write about teaching school. Normally she led business classes and taught women how to type and take shorthand. She was an expert. Sometimes she would make notes in shorthand so only she was able to read them. It was super frustrating because it was like she spoke another language; Denny was certain she lived on another planet, so speaking another language was only to be expected. The question he always wound up asking was one nobody could answer, why would she choose to be with other people instead of him?

Denny only got to visit her once or twice a year and it was always rushed and staged mainly to show others how much she cared for her son. When she would visit, they always took a photo, usually in front of her most recent car. These photos always reminded him that she was leaving soon because she was always dressed to the nines and hugging him as if he were a prop in the photo, an accessory in her life that she would discard when the photo opportunity was over.

Enough of the wallowing in the 'what ifs' of something that could never be, a happy life with his mother, Margo.

Tom was getting excited as they came up to the next town, Las Vegas! He was chattering, "This place is the next big thing! I stopped here on the way out to Denver. We'll gas up, pee, and grab a sandwich at a diner." Tom offered to pay for the food and Denny was extremely thankful for his generosity.

It was great to get out and stretch his legs. Denny wasn't familiar with that particular town, but liked the way it looked, super new and cool. Other than the occasional street dice game in Detroit he didn't know much about gambling or playing cards, but it was all intriguing. While they were at lunch, Tom explained a card game where the goal was to collect cards that added up to 21; he called it blackjack. You tried to guess whether the dealer had cards higher or lower than the cards he gave you and if you guessed correctly, you could win money based on the cash bet you placed. Denny didn't think this would be very hard, and when he was older, he might give it a go.

Las Vegas buzzed with excitement, even though they were only eating lunch, everyone looked like they were going somewhere, like they had a purpose. The weather was amazing, in March it was over 60 degrees. Denny was walking around with no coat, something that would never happen in Michigan this time of year. The women who were walking around were beautiful with every hair in place. The men were dressed impeccably. This made Denny a little self-conscious about his appearance. Tom shrugged it off, they were on a road trip and would be out of here in quick order. Denny had been in the same clothes now for four days, he needed a shave and a shower, he hadn't dare take a whiff of his pits, but was sure he reeked of teen.

After they were fueled up, with food and gas they were back on their way. Tom shared that they were less than five hours from San Bernardino, depending on the road conditions.

PART II
SAN BERNARDINO

Chapter 8

San Bernardino

Denny woke up to Tom exclaiming, "Only one more hour till we are home!" The San Bernardino Valley was quite a sight to behold as they made their way down the Cajon Pass into the basin.

Tom liked living in San Bernardino and would tell anyone who listened how great it was. The house he lived in with his family was located at the base of the San Bernardino Mountain Range. It only took 30 minutes to drive up to the mountains or in less than an hour, Tom's toes could be in the Pacific Ocean at the beach. The view was incredible, and it was a great place to raise his kids. Although his job was a 20-minute drive from his house, he didn't mind it because it gave him time to think and have some alone time.

Tom asked Denny, "So, where does your uncle live?"

Denny offered, "Just over Little Mountain."

"I know where that is, when we're closer, point me where you want me to drop you."

Denny replied, "Tom, if it's okay with you, you can drop me off at a phone booth."

Tom drove over the hill and dropped him off at Marshall and E Street in San Bernardino.

Denny profusely thanked him, and he told Tom, "If you ever need any help and you spot me around town, I would be glad to lend a hand."

Tom parted with this advice, "I wish you well. When it seems like you aren't going anywhere, remember it will always go if you push hard enough."

As Denny walked over to the phone booth, he repeated what Tom had told him which was another nugget of wisdom he was going to store away and think about, like the fact that someone always has it tougher than you do.

Denny sat on a brick wall next to the phone booth and figured out he would call his Aunt Babe first. This would set him back financially, but he had to call her. Denny had a piece of paper that had important phone numbers on it. He hesitated to dial the operator, but sometimes all you need to do is to start something, and before you know it, you're doing it. When the operator came on the line, Denny gave her Babe's number, and she told him it would be two dollars and 50 cents once she picked up. Denny got his change ready.

Aunt Babe came on the line, and she immediately asked, "Where are you?"

Denny told her, "I am in San Bernardino, instead of taking the bus to New Mexico, I hitchhiked out here."

He could hear his aunt sigh and then she told him, "Your Uncle Chuck is out there, maybe you can stay with him for a little bit. Your mom is in Long Beach, do you have something to write with? Let me give you, her address."

Denny told her, "I'm not interested in where she is right now. I came out here to live. I've had enough of her and Bob. I love you, Aunt Babe and I only wanted to tell you where I am. If you hear from Bob or Margo, tell them I am okay, but I want to be on my own."

Babe responded, "I love you Denny and please write to us when you can, please take care of yourself."

Denny told her, "I love you too. Goodbye, I'll write."

Next, he made a call to his Uncle Chuck's optometry office. He was Dr. Charles May, and his office was on Highland Ave. His secretary picked up the call and asked him to please hold and he would be on the line in a minute.

Chuck was surprised to hear Denny on the line. Denny told him he was in San Bernardino. Chuck had always been kind to him, but Denny didn't want to put him out too much. Denny told him the story about what was going on and asked if he could spend one night with him. Chuck said that would be okay, but he really wasn't able to do more than that right now. Denny said he understood and all he needed was a shower and a place to sleep for the night. Chuck said he would pick him up in about an hour and head over to his place.

Denny waved as his Uncle Chuck pulled in. His car was fabulous, although he didn't recognize the model, and his uncle, as always, looked sharp. This made Denny feel like a slouch, but they were at different places in their lives. Chuck hugged him and Denny paused for a second enjoying the contact.

Chuck observed, "Damn, you are getting so tall, son!"

Denny smiled and said, "Thanks for picking me up, I appreciate you letting me spend the night."

Denny got in the back of the car with his bag.

While Chuck drove, he said, "I am not sure if anyone told you, but I am divorcing Nancy. I'm staying in a rental house right now until I'm situated. I have a girlfriend named Fran. She comes over to my house quite a bit but doesn't live with me yet. I have a spare room where you are welcome to spend the night."

Chuck's house was clean. As they walked in the door, Chuck yelled out, "Hi Franny I'm home."

Fran greeted Chuck with a cocktail and a smile. Fran reached out to shake hands, "It's delightful to meet you, Denny, please have a seat. You'll need to tell me all about your adventure. Would you like something to drink?"

Obviously, Chuck had called Fran and let her know the situation. Fran was striking. She looked like the ladies in Las

Vegas; every hair was in place. Denny was afraid to touch anything but took a seat on the couch. Chuck told him, "If you want to put your things in the spare room and take a shower, go ahead, after that we'll have dinner." This was music to Denny's ears as he was anxious to take a shower, shave, and have a long sit down (take a shit).

Denny took this opportunity to duck out and get down to the business of personal hygiene. Everything at the house was so pristine, like it was all new, which given Chuck's imminent divorce, may very well have been the case. Chuck or Fran had put out shampoo and soap for him which smelled like roses. Denny was in the bathroom for about 30 minutes, he then went and picked out his best shirt and pants and made his way back to the living room.

Chuck and Fran were talking and greeted him when he came into the room. Chuck asked Denny, "Does your mom know where you are?"

Denny replied, "No and I don't feel like talking to her at this time. She left me at Bob's, and I know she is living at the beach, but she can live her life and I'll live mine."

Chuck said, "I understand, she has always gone her own way. Even though she is older than me, she acts like she's younger than me. You are awfully young to be on your own, but if that's what you want to do, I will try and help you every once in a while. I do have my hands full with work and I'm still getting back on my feet here. I can't really have you stay here.

Denny nodded. "I will figure out my living situation tomorrow. We've talked a lot about my mom. Can you tell me anything about my dad?"

"Why yes, I can tell you some stuff about your dad, he was a decent guy in many, many, ways. I was taking boys cooking, typing and some other classes in high school. Gene, that's the name he used, came home one day, and checked me out of school. He told me he had changed all my classes, so I got college prep courses. I asked him, what did do you all that for? Gene asked me if I wanted to go to college, because I wasn't going to make it with those sorts of classes. So, he put me into classes to allow me to go to college. It's a damn good thing he did because I didn't have anything to spare when I got to college. That was the biggest favor he ever did for me."

"Once in a while, he would take me to Chicago, because I was going to school in Chicago, he would be driving back and forth between Allegan and Chicago. About every other hour he would have to stop for a beer. I didn't know why he had to stop. Your dad was a real character; he was a gambler too. He could win you over in 30 seconds, he'd win a room in a minute, he was very charismatic. I think he could have sold anything there was to sell, it was just in his nature. He was a super sharp guy, no doubt about it. Because he was supposed to inherit a lot of money when he turned thirty years old, he kind of pooped away his life. Gene didn't give a damn what he did, but he was sharp as they came. I didn't know him that well, but I did know him that way, because I would ride back and forth with him from

Allegan to Chicago. He was always running around someplace. I appreciated him more than anybody else at that time. Your dad owed everybody money he gambled a lot, and he didn't care."

Denny sat for a moment and absorbed all of this. When he was done digesting it all, he joked, "Well, I must have gotten my good looks and charm from him." To which his Uncle Chuck nodded.

With that, they sat down to dinner. The rest of the night was pleasant, and Denny entertained them with the story about Ray doing 100mph from Kansas to Denver. Denny went to bed around 10pm and left Chuck and Fran to have some alone time. As Denny laid in bed on clean, crisp sheets; he was going over what his next moves would be.

Chapter 9

Hitting the Pavement

As Denny woke up, he became aware of pans and plates being moved around in the kitchen. He got up quickly, got dressed, brushed his hair and teeth, and walked out to the living room. Chuck was sitting at the breakfast table eating. A place was set for Denny, and he told him to help himself. Chuck had made quite a bit of eggs and bacon and Denny was happy to finish up any that was left over. Denny knew he would need to leave before Chuck went to work, so after breakfast, he packed up his stuff, along with his freshly washed clothes and decided to go walking around San Bernardino. Before leaving, he hugged Chuck and thanked him for letting stay at his house.

As Denny left, he set out for the area around Little Mountain. If he had to sleep outside, that might be a good place. Chuck and Fran were talking, last night, about it being cold at night, but he was sure it would be California cold, and nothing compared to Michigan cold. As he walked toward the foothills, he noticed how gorgeous it was outside. Even though it was March, it felt like he could wear short sleeves, so he stopped and put his coat in his suitcase.

Finding a job right away was the top priority if he was going to make it on his own. He'd been walking for a couple hours and was on a street called 40th. There had been half a dozen places along the route that he had stopped in looking for a job. At each place he gave his spiel, "Hi, I'm Denny, I just got into town, and I am trying to find a job. Do you have anything, or can you direct me to someone who might need help?" The people he encountered were cordial, but they didn't own the business, and they asked him to come back later in the day to speak to the owner.

Along his walk, were a gas station and a liquor store. The Mobil gas station looked promising, so he stopped and asked if the owner was around. The guy said, "That's me, my name is Fred."

Denny introduced himself, "I'm Denny and I just got here from Michigan. I'm trying to find a job and a place to stay. Do you have anything?"

"Have you ever pumped gas? It's not very hard, as long as you are decent with people, you can even make tips."

"I haven't, but I am sure I can learn."

"How old are you and are you going to school?"

"I'm 13, going on 14. I will be going to school for the next school year, but I need to get a job and a place to live first."

"I can use the help, but I need to pay you under the table. I have a place in the back where you can sleep at night. What do you say I pay you 25 cents an hour and I'll set up a cot in the back for you?"

Denny didn't want to appear to be too excited, he scratched his head and slowly asked, "How much is minimum wage? I heard it was 75 cents an hour."

"Actually for me it's 65 cents because I am a small employer. I can pay 35 cents an hour and you'll have a place to stay, how about that? I'll even provide a uniform for you to wear. My wife can do laundry every couple of days. I live close, up the block here." Fred motioned to the street that headed toward the mountains.

Denny stuck out his hand to shake Fred's hand and said, "It's a deal."

Denny didn't plan on spending a lot of money. Not only did he have eight bucks left from the Golden Police, but he also had his original dollar twenty from Michigan, which brought his fortune to a little over nine dollars.

Fred showed him the room he had in the back. It was okay, smaller than the jail cell he had stayed in, but there was a small window, up high. Denny figured he'd clean up the floor, add a small table for his stuff and it would be good enough for who it was for. Denny put his bag in the room and Fred gave him a key for the door, so he was able to lock it.

The rest of the day Denny followed Fred around and helped him pump gas, wash windshields, check oil, and perform other duties. Denny was tall and none of Fred's uniforms would fit him, so it would be about a week before he had one. Fred explained he was going to be taking payments for gas, so he would need to learn how to run the till, count change, and take gas cards.

Fred smiled and in a serious tone joked, "I am putting a lot of my trust in you. I'm not worried though; I know where you live."

Denny was tired by the end of the day. Fred asked him to dinner at his house, and that sounded wonderful. Going forward he would need to buy some food from the grocery store and figure out how to get around town either by bus or bicycle, but that was a problem for the next day.

Upon arriving at Fred's house, he immediately felt at home. His wife Mable was pleasant. "It's a treat to have a young man around, my son Al is out on his own now. He lives in Texas, where he moved when he got out of the military."

Denny said, "I am on my own now too. I am grateful to your husband here, for giving me a job and a place to bunk. I plan on buying a bicycle when I can afford it."

Mable sat thinking and offered, "Fred, don't we have a bicycle in the shed? If we do, let's let Denny borrow it until he can afford to get one."

Denny asked, "Whose bike, is it?"

"It's Al's old bicycle, we don't have a need for it anymore" she replied.

"Can I buy it from you for ten dollars? I can pay two dollars a week until it's paid off. Does that work?"

They struck a deal and after dinner, Fred dug out the bike and pumped up the tires. He thanked Fred and Mable for everything and biked off to the station to stay in his room.

It was around 10pm when he got back. Denny went into the room and realized he didn't have a blanket or anything, so he put on his long coat to keep warm. Compared to what he was used to, it wasn't that cold, but he was having a tough time winding down to go to sleep.

As he lay on the cot, he took stock of everything that had happened this past week. While he had accomplished quite a bit in a short amount of time, he needed to keep it together. He made a list in his head of the things he had to do in the week ahead. The number one thing was to find a grocery store and buy some affordable food. The food he ate was pretty basic, he would buy some bread, meat for sandwiches, peanut butter, and some other basics.

Just as he started to nod off, he heard a long high-pitched scream, followed by a dog yipping and then more screaming. It was really close, and it scared him. 'What type of creature was making that noise?' The ruckus went on for about an hour.

This was definitely something he needed to ask Fred about, as it was extremely frightening and like nothing he had ever heard before.

He finally fell asleep and didn't wake up until there was a knock at the door. When he opened the door Fred was standing there. Denny was going to do a full day's work, but Fred told him, "Why don't you take a couple hours this morning after the rush and ride around to figure out the lay of the town?"

Denny smiled and said, "Today is going to be an adventure. Where is the best place to buy groceries?"

"Sage's. That place has everything and at a decent price. While you are out and about be careful, as the cops here take truancy seriously. When do you plan on going to school?"

"I need my living situation settled and save up some cash before I do that. I'll enroll in September for the new school year. I think I can steer clear of the cops until then."

Fred took a long time explaining how to navigate San Bernardino.

"This town was laid out by Mormons, and they used a simple grid system. All the north and south streets were important places and names in church history, and the east and west streets were numbers, this made it easy to figure out directions. After the Mormons left, the city changed the names to letters and some of the street names to Sierra Way and Arrowhead, etc., but the basic concept held. In this case, the store is on Baseline and E Street and the way you go there is like this," Fred drew him a little map. "You can go over the mountain here," pointing toward Little Mountain, "to save time, as that turns into E Street, but you would more than likely be walking the bike part of the way as the hill is too steep for most people to ride. I would go out 40th Street to the east and then head south on Sierra Way and then wind your way over to E Street and take it all the way down to Baseline. Be careful, you will be going by the junior high school and the high school that are along the way."

Chapter 10

Lay of the Town

Around 10am, Denny told Fred he would be back in a couple hours. It was great to feel the wind in his hair. He had freshened up a bit and was ready to check out the town. As he biked down 40th Street, he was looking for Sierra Way, that was where he was turning right. Just past Sierra Way to the east was one of those drive-through type corner stores. He stopped there and bought a quart of milk for a nickel. As he rode his bike, Denny noticed all the houses were new. This town was so clean compared to Detroit. Denny wanted to know why the curbs were so high on Sierra Way. In some places they were almost a full foot tall, which was strange.

Denny was able to weave his way through town by using Fred's directions and located Sage's. Once inside, he walked around and liked it. The store had everything including a coffee shop and bakery. After taking a tour he bought some bread, milk, Wheaties, Braunschweiger in the tube, hot dogs, Hershey's chocolate bars, peanut butter, baloney, and Velveeta cheese. No one said anything about him not being in school. Carrying everything back on his bike was difficult, but he made it.

When Denny got back, around 12:30pm, he immediately put his food in his room and started helping out. Fred told him, "I have a small icebox in my office, you can put your stuff in there and later we'll move it into the main garage area." Fred also went over his schedule for work, which would be 7:30am to 11:30am and then 3pm to 7pm. This schedule would allow Fred time to go home for an early lunch and to eat dinner with Mable before coming back to close the station for the night.

Fred came back to close up after he went home from dinner and sat with Denny for a couple minutes. He asked, "How was your first day?"

Denny said, "I had a good day, thanks for helping me out so much, I truly appreciate it. I was having a bad time with my stepdad, and I had to leave."

"What you are trying to do here, being on your own, is going to be rough, but I will help you if I can. This may not be a permanent arrangement, but hopefully you will be able to get on your feet with a little bit of luck."

"I appreciate the help. I do have one question though, last night I heard howling, and it scared the shit out of me. Can you tell me what that was?"

Fred laughed, "You'll hear them almost every night. Those are coyotes. Welcome to the southwest! They run in packs and when you hear them yipping, they have typically killed something. They tend to feed on chickens, stray dogs, and anything else they can scavenge. They are super smart."

Denny laughed nervously and thanked him for the information. That night alone in his room, he heard the coyotes partying again with their ominous chatter.

Chapter 11

Margo's New Life in Long Beach

Margo had just heard from her brother Chuck, her sister Babe, and Bob all in the same day. What a Saturday! All she wanted to do was go to the beach and enjoy her day off. Margo, Jeanna, and her kids, were going to the beach after Jeanna got off work.

Jeanna and Margo had lived together for two years, and things were going well. They hit a groove in their relationship that Margo hadn't found with any of her husbands or other male companions.

This wasn't the first time she had the pleasure of female companionship. During the roaring twenties before the depression, she and her friend Vera had experimented in intimate relations. They were flappers and Margo remembered that time as one of the happiest of her life. She loved the clothes, the parties, the speakeasies, the sex, and the thrill of drinking in everything that was forbidden, including alcohol. Something about that time in her life brought out her true self. Margo could never recapture the carefree feeling of being freshly out of high school, going to college without responsibilities; she longed for those times. Back in the day when she was super-hot and beautiful. She ran through men like a field of flowers picking the ones who promised to support her lifestyle and tastes.

Because she was the oldest, Margo was afforded many advantages. She obtained a college degree and was qualified to teach. Winning the state championship in Michigan for typing 120 words per minute was always a good brag on her resume and secured her many teaching jobs. Her unique looks, chestnut red hair, and a stature of five feet ten inches made men fall in love with her at the drop of a hat.

During the Great Depression she worked for Luzier Cosmetics and made decent money, but always kept these earnings for herself. For the most part she was self-sufficient during this time. Heading out of the Depression she took a job in Port Huron at the high school where she taught typing and shorthand.

After she married Gene (Eugene) Dulin, things changed for her. They spent about a year together, but Gene left her and Denny on Christmas Day, 1938. She knew the next husband she found needed to be older, more settled down and kind of a schmuck, so she married Bob. She gave him enough attention so he would satisfy her need for someone to take care of Denny. Make no mistake, while she was married to Bob, she had several affairs and was gone for weeks at a time.

The recent development with Denny running away might derail everything if she didn't quash it.

Where she lived in California, was perfect. They were two blocks from the beach. Margo worked at a business college teaching stenography. Jeanna was a cashier at Long Beach Community Hospital. Although Margo worked during the week and Jeanna worked odd hours, both of them were typically off on Sunday. Jeanna had two girls and even though this was burdensome sometimes, they made it work.

Margo was sick of Denny's shit. She did the best she could, but a woman has needs and sometimes having a son gets in the way of those needs and her fun.

Over the years she realized that she was not a good mother, but she always put up a matronly front. She made a production, a show if you will, for everyone to witness how much she cared for him. Her family had her number and understood she was a shit mom; so did Bob and Denny. Yet whenever she spoke with people about her son, she showed off the latest photo and said how proud she was of him, made up some lie about recently talking to him and shared a story about what he was doing presently. Truth be told, she didn't have a fucking clue about her Denny.

Another truth that she would never tell anyone is that she didn't care about anyone but herself. The most important person to Margo was Margo, plain and simple.

As she sat outside smoking in the sunshine, she was trying to figure out how to find someone else to take care of Denny. For now, she wasn't going to do anything. She was going adopt a wait-and-see position until someone in the family pushed her to do something. The school she was teaching at had classes that would end in June. If she was able to bide her time till then, she could figure out a plan. The thing she liked about teaching was that she had a break of anywhere from one to three months, depending on what the school curriculum was.

One thing that Margo never really got out of her system was herself. Even as she sat on the porch thinking about her son, she wasn't really thinking about him, only about what this situation meant for her. She also decided not to tell Jeanna about what was going on.

Sure, she knew Margo had a son, but she still thought he was living with Bob. Margo had told Jeanna that Denny lived with Bob because he liked living there. 'Gracious Margo' was accommodating the wishes of her son, even though she would rather he live with her. Denny had run away a couple times before never making it far, but last summer he made it all the way to Babe's house.

Margo held back information like this from people she was close to. She would never admit things how many times she had been married, what her true age was, and sometimes she lied to her advantage to procure favor or jobs. Her biggest lies were always about her son and their relationship. People never checked on things like basic facts, and these were generally easy to conceal.

At this point, she would do nothing except smoke another cigarette. Later she would go inside and figure out what Jeanna's daughters wanted for lunch. Margo had been focusing lately on teaching the six-year-old girl how to make peanut butter sandwiches, so she could fend for herself and her four-year-old sister.

Chapter 12

Some Hard Truths for Bob

It was about two weeks after Denny arrived, still living at the gas station, when Fred asked him to come to the phone. Denny was perplexed, but came over and answered, "Hello."

On the other end of the line was an old familiar, unwelcome voice, "Hi Denny, it's Bob. I happened to be in town and wanted to stop by. I heard you work at a gas station, and I have the address. Is that alright?"

"Sure, what time are you coming over, I don't have a break until 11:30am."

"I'll be over then."

Denny hung up the phone and stared at Fred who was watching him closely.

"That was weird, my stepdad wants to come visit me, he came out here all the way from Michigan, what the hell?"

"It's almost the weekend, so if you need a couple days off, go ahead, I don't have plans."

"Thanks, I'm not sure what he wants, or what is going on."

Around noon, Bob pulled up in his car, so Denny guessed he must have driven out to California. Bob parked and got out, hat in hand and glanced sheepishly at Denny. "How have you been?"

"I've been okay, this place is way better than freezing my balls off in Michigan." Denny made it a point to be a dick.

"I can see that; do you think you could take a couple days off and go for a little trip with me up the coast to Santa Barbara? I would like to apologize for how I treated you and help you out a little."

"When were you thinking about going?"

"We could leave tonight and be back by Sunday night. I figured we might go fishing and sightseeing."

"Sure, let me talk to my boss and I will let you know in a minute."

After re-confirming the time off with Fred, he informed Bob he was able to go, but he absolutely had to be back by Sunday night.

Bob took off with a promise to be back around 7:30pm. When Fred came back after his dinner, he said, "While you are gone with him, keep in mind it's only for two days and you'll be back here in no time. Try and keep your cool and see what he has to say."

"I will, I'm not aware what his angle is or why he would drive all the way out here to visit me."

Bob, true to his word, came by to pick him up on time, and in a couple minutes they were on their way. Denny had taken precautions, he made sure he had enough cash to take the bus back if needed or use his favorite hitchhiking thumb as his exit plan. He had no qualms about leaving Bob anywhere along the trip if he got to be too much of an asshole.

What struck Denny odd was that Bob was being very polite and on his best behavior. It was almost as if Bob had missed his companionship. After all, he didn't have many friends and now he was in his house all by himself. Denny tuned into what he was saying.

"So, how did you make it out to California?"

"I hitched out here; it was definitely interesting. How did you know where to find me?"

"Oh, I talked to your Uncle Chuck, he's the one who told me where you were staying, have you talked to your mom since you've been out here?"

"Last I heard she was shacked up with Jeanna in Long Beach, but beyond that, no, I haven't spoken to her, why, have you?"

"No, she hasn't called or written since you left."

'Bingo! That's why he's here,' he was the only bait Bob had to attract her back to him. No Denny, no contact. What a pathetic little old man. Denny was kind of tired, so he laid his head on the window and took a nap.

When he woke up, they were pulling into an all-night diner in Santa Barbara. They ate a quick dinner and then went to a motel and spent the night.

Bob's heart was set on going to the Santa Barbara Mission, which was beautiful, but Denny could only appreciate the beauty of the area. Although Bob was keen on the missions, he had no interest in crosses, bells, or other religious trappings. He thought, 'How absurd that all of this was built by the Indians who were pressed into service by the padres. All in the name of God.' Denny was relatively sure they were doing just fine before the Spaniards and the white man came along and 'civilized' this area under the guise of religion and greed.

After a while they went down to the main part of Santa Barbara, had some stranger take their photo in front of the courthouse, and ate lunch on the wharf. Bob had this wild idea about fishing for the rest of the day, so they went down to the marina and were able to go out for the afternoon. Denny caught a couple of fish, but he threw them back because they weren't prepared to cook or store them.

That night they had dinner at the other seafood restaurant on the wharf and, while they ate, Bob poured his heart out to Denny.

"I sure do miss having you around. It's not the same without you and I am very sorry about pushing you around like I did. You didn't deserve that or being locked in the basement."

Denny pushed it aside, "Bob, I'm sorry too that you treated me that way, but I think your major problem is that you are still in love with Margo. You need to let that go. She is a man-eater, and she will never be faithful. I think the sooner you realize that the better for you."

Bob admitted, "I agree with you, she has this way about her where she can suck me back in, even though I swear I am done with her."

Denny pondered this and imparted wisdom to Bob that was well beyond his years, "I'm sure you recognize, she is a whirling vortex that sucks in everything in her path. She'll be upon you before you can comprehend what's happening. When she spits you out, you're broken, or your shit is broken, and you have nothing left. She is all consuming, it's better to steer clear of her and avoid all contact if possible. She is a consumer in more ways than one."

Bob sat for a long moment and thought about what Denny had said.

"I agree, I think I will leave her alone. I have spent the best part of ten years chasing that woman and for what? Don't get me wrong, I love you like a son, but she has brought out the worst in me."

Sometimes things are better left unsaid, so Denny stopped short of telling him he loved him—and that he had almost killed him a couple weeks ago.

The next day they went to Ventura and took a leisurely drive south along the coast and then headed back to San Bernardino, where Bob dropped Denny off around six at night. They said their farewells and Denny hoped that would be the last he heard from Bob Ertell.

Chapter 13

Survival Mode

One thing Denny learned about San Bernardino was that nearly everyone had fruit trees on their property, especially in the Arrowhead Farms area. The homeowners couldn't eat all the fruit that came off the trees and often it went to waste. Denny was starting to learn the names of fruit trees. Lately he had been eating a lot of oranges, grapefruit and, on occasion, lemons. He also learned that if you offered to help and pick the fruit, the people who owned the trees would pay you in fruit. They would ask him about his situation, and he would tell them his family was barely making ends meet and he was trying to help any way he could by gathering unused fruit. This story endeared him to people, and he usually wound up receiving free stuff. Occasionally people would feed him. This was a much better way of getting free fruit instead of just taking it.

Peanut butter or baloney sandwiches were Denny's sustenance most days. The odd treat was when he was invited to someone's house for a meal. Invitations were few and far between, but usually every couple of weeks he had a home-cooked meal. He would on occasion be invited to Fred's for dinner or sometimes Fred would bring back leftovers when he came to close up the station. Fred let Denny take a shower over at his place once or twice a week after work. Most of the time Denny would either hose off out behind the station or in a pinch if it was too cold, he would use the large sink in the garage.

Denny thought Fred was a good person and he asked him for quite a bit of advice about the basics of life and how things worked while he was working at the station. Their relationship was symbiotic. Fred got to take breaks, go home, and eat dinner with his wife and Denny was able to have cash to survive.

Hobos were a great source of information. They hung out at the rail yards and also up in the foothills. They also frequented the liquor store next to the gas station. One of these travelers told him about a huge, abandoned vineyard north of the airport and the grapes would be in season over the summer. Coming from Michigan, having fruit to pick almost year-round was unheard of. Denny relied on this for some of his food.

He was trying not to spend money on things that people would give to him, or he could acquire for free. On Bob's recent trip out, he had given him $20, which brought his savings to over $50.

The more affluent area of San Bernardino was over by the golf course. Doctors, lawyers, and professional people lived in this area. Whenever they threw stuff away, it was because they didn't want it anymore, not because it was damaged or unusable. The key to digging in the trash was to do it when everyone was asleep. People left their garbage in the alley behind their house. Trash picking involved going around town at night. This also meant he would encounter coyotes, possums, stray cats, racoons, and the occasional bobcat slinking around.

Coyotes ran in packs. They could be found on the golf course and in the foothills, and they were sneaky. Denny watched them every once in a while, and figured out the reasons coyotes yip is because they caught some dinner or were signaling to their mates, so Fred's theory was correct. To Denny they sounded like they were throwing their own little party. The way they worked as a team was interesting. The pack always had a lead coyote and trailing behind them would be two more, and a couple behind them. The first one would turn around and adopt a playful pose, tap its front paws on the ground. The other two would also 'play.' If it was a dog they were stalking, it might think it was playtime too, and then the pack would pounce and kill the animal.

On more than one occasion he watched a solitary coyote leap on top of fence, grab a pet, and leave as quickly as it had come into the yard. Many cats and small dogs were snatched up under the cover of darkness and little Susy would never find out what happened to her tabby Buttons. Denny tried to intervene a couple of times, and was successful in thwarting two attacks, but people didn't learn and continuously left their pets outside in this coyote-eat-dog environment.

Most people were oblivious to the wildlife in their surroundings. Just out of sight, lurking in the foothills were mountain lions. He had seen one of these cougars when he was biking through the abandoned vineyards at dusk on an old tractor road. The big cat was perched on a hillside ledge about 15 feet off the ground and was ready to pounce and feed on unsuspecting prey. 'Was he being stealthily stalked?' That was the first time he had seen a mountain lion so close. Since the sighting he steered clear of the undeveloped areas of the foothills in the early morning and late at night.

Also, in the vineyards he had come across snakes straddling the width of the road like a roadblock. He had turned around more than once rather than contend with these cold-blooded reptiles. Sometimes they were in the sage brush and when it was hot, they could be found sunning themselves on rocks. Rattlesnakes were something Denny avoided altogether.

That particular night he was focused on his cache. He had scored a decent sports coat that fit him well and a small wicker end table, just the right size for a lamp, but small enough to strap on the back of his bike.

Chapter 14

Thinking

Denny did his fair share of daydreaming at work. As he stood pumping gas, he was watching another plane coming in for a landing. The gas station was the perfect vantage point for watching planes. It was at the end of the runway for the San Bernardino airport. This airport was busy with small planes. Denny wasn't sure how long the airport had been around, but Southern California was the perfect place for flying.

As he daydreamed, he wondered what it was like to be a pilot. He didn't want to fly in a war; he just wanted to feel what it would be like to fly a small plane anywhere he wanted to go. It had to be quicker than his bicycle or even a car.

Fred told him that once or twice a year, someone missed the runway and crashed. Usually, crashes happened because the planes were too low on their final approach to the field, and most of the pilots walked away with minor injuries. Denny hadn't seen one crash yet and didn't want to. One day he would like to go over to the airport and check it out. It might be fun talking to pilots and listening to their stories.

Being in constant survival mode was hard but it was better than his previous situation of living with Bob. Denny was grateful to be able to live on his own and thankful that he didn't need to endure his mom's platitudes when he talked to her. If he was going to be let down by anyone, it would be himself. Denny's Uncle Chuck and Uncle Milt gave him his mom's phone number and told him she would accept a collect call if he would please call her. He hadn't. She was a selfish bitch and could keep her 'collect call' money.

Denny got two days off a week and was eager for summer to come so he could make some friends. A couple of kids would go over to the liquor store and buy candy and then come by the station to shoot the shit with him. The place they talked about a lot was the Perris Hill Plunge. Denny was thinking during the midday break of four hours that he would get some swimming in when the pool opened for the summer.

Chapter 15

San Bernardino Is Part of the Desert

Jesus Christ, it was fucking hot. No one said how hot San Bernardino got in the summer. It was like a blast furnace. At work the only way for Denny to keep cool was to drink lots of water and hose his head down with water every hour or so. If he didn't, he would feel sick.

His clothing was key to surviving the heat. He wore a hat to keep the sun off his head and a long-sleeved shirt so his arms wouldn't burn from the sun. Sweating in his shirt was like turning on a swamp cooler. Any breeze that would blow through the shirt would cool the sweat. Sometimes he would flap the tail of the shirt back and forth to move air over his torso. It was counter-intuitive, but a highly effective way to cool down. The real heat hit at 2pm, when a hot wind would kick up in the valley usually caused by trade winds that came off the Pacific Ocean.

The kids who had been dropping by the station were Terry LaMere, Billy Soristo, and Jim Christie. Most days they would come by and invite Denny to the Plunge. If they were too lazy to bike to the Plunge, they would visit a couple closer reservoirs where they could swim and quickly cool off on particularly sweltering days.

The Plunge was where the action was. It cost 15 cents to swim. Denny had a cheap swimsuit and loved hanging out and swimming. The kids that went to this pool were well to do and came from the new areas of San Bernardino, over by the country club.

The girls at the Plunge were something special. Denny felt being in his swim trunks offered him a level playing field when it came to the girls. He was dressed like all the other kids. Denny had a light brown tan because he was outside so much, and his hair had lightened up quite a bit over the summer.

Denny made small talk with the teens at the pool, and as always didn't give up too much information about his past. The lifeguards would occasionally yell at his crew for roughhousing too much. He liked to be with his crew, but more and more his attentions were fixed on girls. Sure, some of the girls had boyfriends, but he was polishing his flirting skills. As long as he was respectful, he was able to practice without getting into trouble.

One of the girls who went to the pool quite a bit was Becky. She had a group of girls she hung with. She was aged 15 and fabulous. Her suit was cut the way Denny preferred, leaving some of her curves to the imagination. She was older than him, but he understood she was into him, because she had complimented him on his piercing blue eyes. He could only spend two hours each time he went to the pool, due to work. Most of the time he would swim for a while, hang out with the boys for a few and then cruise around and see who was there to chat up. If Becky was there, he would stay in the pool by where she hung out and talk to her. If not, he would walk around trying to project a calm, cool, collected demeanor.

It took quite an effort to be cool and he kept practicing brooding looks and various other side glances. Denny was good at hiding his feelings, so anytime his shyness threatened to surface, he would push it back down and remain nonchalant and hip. One of his tricks was to move his eyebrows independently. This always made the girls laugh when it was deployed as a skillful flirting technique.

Denny wasn't looking for a lot of action, just a little petting and kissing for now. His mom's antics taught him how to recognize a girl who might siderail him and wreak havoc; he only wanted to have a little fun.

It was hard to explain how badly he wanted a motorcycle or even a motorized bike, like a Whizzer. His whole body ached for it. It would be something that would elevate his cool vibe because the bicycle wouldn't cut if for much longer. He added a few things to make his bike better, but it was strictly transportation, from point A to point B. Denny treated his bike very well because it was his freedom ticket. The boys he rode with would pull stupid stunts and jump curbs, do wheelies and such. After Denny dumped it, the first time, he focused more on taking care of his ride and tried not to fuck up his only transportation. Things were a little more serious for him than his friends and the stakes were much higher.

On the way to the pool and back, the guys would joke around, sometimes they would take detours such as biking across the golf course or take a short cut through the cemetery. When they left the pool, they made sure they were dripping wet, but by the time they hit 40th Street, they were completely dry. They would, on occasion, stop by a house, hose off, and be back on their bikes before anyone was the wiser.

During their trips they would find little treasures. These trinkets were small bits that nobody would ever miss. Their previous places of prominence were holes in pockets, the front of a dress loosely tethered by frayed thread or the hand of a distracted child. Pennies, jacks, die, buttons, paperclips, single-clip earrings and other bits and bobs were lost, but thankfully found by the boys. When an item was found it was placed in a tin for safekeeping. Sometimes when they stopped, they would open the box and take inventory of the treasure.

It was on one of these summer bike rides that they decided to sit under the shade of a giant tree after hosing down. They were sitting on the high curbs of Sierra Way when they heard some large black birds squawking in the tree. Denny thought they were ravens or crows. He noticed they would drop the seeds from the tree in the street on purpose. This went on for a while. Each time a car passed, one or two of the birds would fly over and make a drop as well as inspect what they had dropped previously.

After about ten cars went by and when the proper signal, a squawk, was given, they all gathered in the street and picked up the remains of what had been run over. They sat and watched the birds for about 30 minutes, too lazy to climb back on their bikes. Billy went out to examine what was being dropped in the street, cautiously making sure no cars were coming and came back with a shell. Denny studied it and said, "I'll be damned if that isn't a walnut shell! These birds were certainly clever. They have a food source right there and were letting the cars do all the work for them."

Denny would never think about birds the same way again. Especially crows and ravens. Over time they had adapted to work smarter not harder and that was amazing. 'How long they had been doing this? Did this start with the covered wagons when the Mormons came to San Bernardino? Did they lay out nuts the same way, hoping the metal covered wagon wheels would run them over—or was this something that started more recently with the invention of the automobile?' Either way Denny made a note to take this as a lesson and work smarter, not harder. A solution could be simple and right in front of your face, and if you don't slow down to check out what's going on around you, you will never discover them.

Sometimes they went to swim in the reservoir up at the top of Electric Ave, which was named after the old Pacific Electric

Railcars that ran up to the Arrowhead Springs Resort. They would follow a road along the foothills next to the old vineyards. On this road they would pick grapes and eat them as a snack. They were always watching for snakes when they were out in the fields.

The boys weren't supposed to swim in the reservoir, but they did it anyway. The only reason Denny thought it was okay to swim there was because he had looked at it when it was dry, and he hadn't seen any hidden threats or machinery. Every once in while someone would chase them off, but for the most part they were left alone. They had to be careful and make sure they knew how to climb in and out of the reservoir safely. They stayed away from the deep end which was to the south of the reservoir. The shallow end, near the foothills, was sloped and provided an easy entry and exit.

Denny liked this place because it was closer to work, easy to get to for a quick dip, but alas, there were no girls there. The reservoir had a dirt bottom, so they had to hose off when they were done swimming. Denny was always careful around water because one time he almost drowned. He was confident enough with his and his friends' swimming skills to know they would be safe. He had been taught the buddy system a few years back, at camp and the boys agreed to use the buddy system after Denny explained it to them.

When Denny first went to the reservoir, the dirt bottom reminded him of the day he almost drowned at the lake. It was a sunny day, at Camp Rankin on Lake Huron and he was swimming with a group of boys. His mom had dropped him off that day for summer camp. Being new to camp and not knowing anyone could be intimidating, but he made quick friends as he usually did and hung out with some boys for the day. They were all roughly around the age of eight. Denny could swim, but he wasn't great at it. The best he could do was dog paddle, but it was enough to get out of the lake, he would paddle over to the ladder, climb up and wait in line and jump in the water again, back, and forth until it was time to leave.

Things were going well—until he got pushed in. All of a sudden Denny couldn't tell which way was up or down. The ladder wasn't visible, so he wasn't sure where he was in relation to it. Lake platforms were different from pools because there were no sides to cling to. Finally, he was able to pop his head up and see the ladder, but it was so far away. Because he couldn't touch the lake bottom, it was a real struggle. Bobbing up and down, catching his breath and paddling, was making him tired and he was starting to panic.

All of a sudden, Denny remembered something his Uncle John had told him. "If for some reason you can't swim, don't panic. Turn on your back by tilting your head back, your legs will come up and you will float." John practice this with him more than once for which Denny was eternally grateful.

As soon as Denny did this, his legs lifted up and he was floating on his back. As he was catching his breath he shouted, "Help! Help!"

The lifeguard came over and plucked him out of the lake. After that day, Denny swore that he would learn how to swim very well, and by the end of the summer, he had learned a couple strokes and was a good swimmer.

Chapter 16

Earthquake!

On July 21, 1952, at 4:55am, California rocked young Denny's world. He was jolted out of bed at the station by a shaking force. At first, he thought a car hit the station. He got up, darted around, and didn't see anything through the garage windows. It really bugged him that he couldn't locate what caused the commotion. Going back to sleep took quite a while, his nerves were shot, and his adrenaline was keeping him awake.

As soon as Fred came in, he asked, "Hey, did you feel the earthquake this morning?"

Denny replied, "Is that what the fuck that was? I thought I was losing my mind. I convinced myself it was my imagination."

"Was that the first time you've been through an earthquake? Oh damn, that's right you aren't from here!"

"Yes, it was, and I thought a car had crashed into the building. I didn't know what the hell was happening."

Fred sat down and educated Denny about earthquakes and how the north end of San Bernardino was mostly built on the San Andreas fault. "If you go closer to the foothills, the actual fault line is visible. This fault is responsible for most of the quakes in Southern California and it has many faults that feed into it, kind of like a river. The earth has layers, called tectonic plates, that sometimes slide together, and the friction causes the earth to shake." Fred reassured Denny, "Don't worry about them. If the ground starts shaking, especially if you are inside, stand up and walk outside. The main danger in an earthquake is from buildings and things falling on you. Don't sweat it. As long as you remember to go outside, you'll be fine."

Denny thought 'that's all well and fine, but I am still going to worry about earthquakes.' It was one more thing on the list of things to worry about.

All day, people were super animated talking about the earthquake. It gave them something in common with everyone else. This included all the folks coming in to buy gas. People started the conversations on that day with, "Hey that was some earthquake this morning, huh?' or "Did you feel the big one?" or his favorite was "Hey, did we just have another earthquake?"

Customers who had been listening to the radio told him the earthquake was centered in Tehachapi. Over ten people had died so far, and it measured 7.3 in magnitude, which was second only to the San Francisco earthquake in 1906. Denny got a crash course in earthquakes, and he had learned way more than he cared to know.

The guys came by and were chattering excitedly about the quake as they biked over to swim, and they were shocked to hear that Denny had never been through an earthquake before. It made him feel a little better that this was the strongest quake any of them had ever felt and they all admitted they had been scared too.

The pool was buzzing with talk about the earthquake. It was kind of weird that a shared experience could bring kids out of their shells. Everyone was talking to everyone else about the earthquake. Denny didn't want to experience another earthquake, perish the thought, but it was fascinating to observe this firsthand. The feeling of inclusion in that shared experience was interesting and Denny understood why people liked to be part of something. Surely this didn't happen every time an earthquake hit, but it was great to be able to meet new people and share a common bond. He wished it was more like this all the time, minus the earthquake.

The rest of the summer passed without any more earthquakes or other disasters. As a matter of fact, his birthday, August 27, passed without so much as a howdy fucking do from anyone. Denny chose not to make a fuss about it, and he kept his birthday to himself. As he lay in bed considering what turning 14 meant for him, he was thankful he had made it five, nearly six months on his own. When he took inventory of his savings, he was pleased to see he had 100 bucks, which was not bad for being a runaway. He was going to talk to Fred about how to keep his money safe. Next up for him would be to hunker down and go to the school and enroll. Fred, his Uncle Chuck, and pretty much every other adult he ran into had been preaching this to him, so he was going to register about a week after it started. He didn't want to deal with all the registration madness that usually came with the start of a new school season.

Chapter 17

Another Day, Another School

Denny asked, "Where is the school?" Fred wrote the address on a piece of paper, handed it to Denny and said it was located over by Highland and E Street and that he passed by it every time he went to Sage's to buy groceries.

Fred and Denny worked out an abbreviated schedule where he would work from 3pm-7pm and, instead of having one day off at the weekend off, he would work eight hours Saturday and Sunday and be off all day on Tuesdays. This would still give him around 30 hours a week, so he was able to keep saving and still help Fred out.

As Denny was leaving, he yelled, "I'll be back when school is over."

Denny wasn't sure how he was going to play it when he got to the school office, but he was going to be creative. Following his usual path to Sage's he crossed over a couple of streets once he got below the foothills and wound up on E Street and took it all the way to Highland Avenue. Sure as shit, there was the Arrowview Junior High School on the right-hand side.

Denny brought the bike up to the windows where the entrance was and put it in the bike rack. To protect his only asset, he was going to need a lock, but he would chance it this one time. As he walked into the office, he braced himself.

The secretary sitting at the desk smiled and asked, "How can I help you?"

"My name is Denny Ertell, and I would like to register for school. I am out here living with my uncle, and he is at work, but he told me to come down here and see if I might at least be able to come to class today. I got here yesterday. I am supposed take the paperwork back to him, he'll fill it out and I'll bring it back tomorrow." He was able to say this all-in-one breath, making sure he got the whole lie out before she said anything.

"This is highly unusual, letting you come to class on your first day without having the paperwork filled out, but since you are here, let me see what I can do." She got up from her desk, spoke with someone, came back, and asked a few more questions.

"What was the last school you attended and what grade were you in? What is your birth date?"

"I attended Ferndale High School, but in Michigan, the ninth graders went to high school. I understand out here, they go to junior high school."

She filled out some paperwork, with the info he provided, and from what Denny guessed it was enough for him to get started because she called a counselor to help him set up his classes.

The counselor introduced himself as Mr. Reed and asked Denny what he wanted to be when he got out of high school. In his head, he thought, 'well, I would like to be alive.' What he actually told the counselor was a lie because Denny didn't have a fucking clue what he wanted to do.

"I'd like to be a mechanic."

"We don't have auto shop here, but we have a metal working shop."

"That works for me."

"Does your mom make you lunch? Can she afford to feed you?"

"No, I am living in a room at my uncle's house, and I fend for myself quite a bit."

"The PTA, Parent-Teacher Association, here can provide lunch to kids whose parents can't afford to feed them."

Denny was sure he was sizing him up, appraising his clothes, shoes and personal hygiene and had already decided that he would be a perfect candidate for this program. This would be a great help to Denny, to make it on his own. Mr. Reed gave him a free lunch pass for the week and asked him to come to the office every week to pick up a new one. He also printed the school schedule and gave him a couple carbon copies of it to show his teachers.

They stood up and Mr. Reed told him he was going to give him a tour of the campus. Denny remembered his bike was outside and asked if there was a place to store it. Mr. Reed directed him to bring the bike along and they would put it in the bike cage. The cage was only open in the morning to store bikes and opened again when school was let out to prevent the bikes from being stolen. Denny wheeled his bike into a packed cage, sandwiched it in with all the others and hoped it would be there at the end of the day.

Denny followed as the counselor described how the school was laid out, showed him the cafeteria, and took him to his assigned locker. Denny practiced the combo a couple times, and then he was good to go. Because Denny was a little late, the counselor took him to his second class which was English.

Denny had been to so many schools he never sweated the first day. He always rolled with the flow. As he walked into the class, he realized he didn't have a pencil or a notebook but would try and borrow at least a sheet of paper and a pencil from someone. Mr. Reed introduced him to the class and to his teacher, whose name he promptly forgot.

The class was a typical classroom, but the teacher was not. She should have been a movie star. She wasn't like any of the teachers in Michigan. He could never imagine her grabbing a metal ruler and whacking it across his knuckles. She was about five feet ten inches tall and wore a beautiful blue suit with a white blouse. Her strawberry blonde hair curled and fell on her shoulders ever so slightly. Her glasses were on the desk but wasn't wearing them. Her eyes were a beautiful hazel color. It was at this moment Denny realized he was gawking at her, so he waved at the class and said, "Pleased to meet you." He went and sat at the closest empty desk.

The teacher asked him, "Denny, can you tell the class a little bit about yourself?"

In situations like this, it was best to give very little information. He always tried to keep his background vague and a bit of a mystery. The less information kids found out about your personal life the less ammunition they had to be mean. Denny offered, "I just moved here from Detroit, Michigan and I am not used to this heat. I feel like I might melt." This made everyone laugh and he felt like he got off on the right foot.

The day flew by and before long, Denny found it was time to head back to work.

Later that night after Fred got back from dinner, Fred helped him with the school paperwork. The address they used was Fred's brother's address. "I did this because if they come looking for you, they won't find you and it might come in handy if you decide to ditch school." With that he winked and said he would see Denny tomorrow.

Chapter 18

Routine

Denny settled in at school and got into a routine after a couple months. His buddies all lived in an eight-block area and because Billy was the farthest away, he would sweep by the gas station for Denny and then together they would head over to pick up Terry and Jim.

It was on one of these rides that Denny almost got clipped by a car. While nothing physically happened to him, it did bring back old memories that he ruminated about for the rest of the day.

Denny remembered two separate incidents. One had to do with his tricycle and the other with a car. It was interesting how the mind worked to pull memories into the present day triggered by a seemingly unrelated event.

Denny's first vivid memory was when he was about three years old. For some unknown reason, he rode his trike down the steps of Bob's front porch. On the way down, he bit his tongue so hard Bob had to take him to the hospital. He remembered this because he bled all the way along the walkway and on the steps as he ran back into the house. This memory was triggered every time he walked out the front door of that house. The drops of blood stained the concrete stairs and walkway and remained visible as a permanent reminder of his trip down the stairs. Denny also believed that biting his tongue almost in half enabled him to roll his tongue into an O shape or fold it horizontally.

When he was four years old, Denny was focused on kicking his ball around the yard. Alone, with no adult supervision around, he'd chased his ball into the street a couple times. The last time he ran after it he remembered glancing up and seeing a car coming at him. As he darted back toward the house, his leg was grazed by the car and he fell, hitting his head on the pavement.

The next thing he remembered a man was carrying him over to the lawn. The man sat with him for a minute as he woke up, and said, "Hey little man, can you walk?" Denny didn't say anything but stood up and showed him he was able to take a couple steps, even though he winced a little and his knees were all scraped up. As he stood on the grass, the man dusted him off, wiped off his knees with his handkerchief then turned, got back in his car, and drove off.

Remembering this incident made Denny feel bad for his younger self. This was a close call; he could have been killed and no-one cared or even knew about it except Denny. No one even asked about his scraped knees.

It was a wonder he was still alive when he thought back on all the shit he had put up with and been through. Denny pushed these memories aside by the end of that day and did the only thing he could—look ahead, not behind.

It was hard for Denny to stay focused on school when he was trying to survive. His grades basically sucked. His best grade was in PE, which was a B, his shop class grade was a C, and the rest were D's. He was in love with his English teacher, but he was so distracted by her in that class, he barely listened to her instructions which earned him a solid D in her class. Denny believed she was his first love, but Becky ran a close second.

Terry, Jim, and Billy were in a couple of his classes, but the metal shop was where they really had fun. They had to be careful not to get too carried away or they would catch the ire of Mr. Hamilton, their shop teacher. He was from Alabama and was strict. There was a heavy wooden paddle he kept behind his desk, and he was known to use it on occasion.

School was the same anywhere Denny went. It was like the ocean. The rich kids were very gossipy, mean, and cliquey, like dolphins and seals, bouncing around making waves. The everyday students were passing through, not making waves in the smoother water, schools of fish, such as minnows or anchovies, minding their own business. At the deeper depths, in the shadows of the reefs were the outcasts, bullies, and bottom feeders, these were the sharks, electric eels and crustaceans. Denny considered himself to be near the bottom, but not completely on the ocean floor; he could have been a shark or a stingray, but not a jellyfish, nope, not a jellyfish.

Denny was thankful that he got a free lunch, as this was usually the best meal of the day for him. His counselor at school, Mr. Reed, seemed to be aware what was going on with Denny and he continued to offer him free lunch passes, as well as turn him onto any programs that were meant for the needy. He was the one who told him about the Salvation Army and Goodwill and how they had nice clothes for cheap.

During his time at school, Denny would catch himself daydreaming about building a motorcycle from a 'bike in a box kit.' These were World War II surplus motorcycles that had been disassembled and shipped in a box. That's what he was saving up for. Denny hoped when the time came, Fred would share some of his mechanical expertise with him about how to put it together.

Chapter 19

Holidays, 1952

For Christmas, Denny was invited to his Uncle Chuck and Aunt Fran's house. His Grandpa May and his wife Hazel would be coming, along with his Uncle Milt and Aunt Madeline and cousin Sharon. His grandpa recently moved to California and lived in Colton, just a block away from San Bernardino, off Highland Avenue. Denny asked if Margo was going to go, and Chuck said they had begged her off due to Chuck and Fran's recent wedding. Denny accepted the invitation since he didn't want to feel sorry for himself like he did on his birthday.

When he got to Chuck's, only his grandpa and Hazel had arrived. Denny said his hellos to Chuck and Fran and gave them hugs. As soon as the pleasantries were done, his grandpa called Denny over to sit with him.

His grandpa took a good long look at Denny and asked "How have you been doing? You are getting so tall."

"I made it through the past nine months on my own. I'm doing alright. It's been hard, but I am going to school and living in the back of a gas station right now."

"I'm so sorry your mom has been such a mess. I don't understand where we went wrong. She started out ambitious, but during college, she turned into a harpy. You weren't alive in the 1920s, but it was a free for all."

"I think I know what a harpy is, but what happened with my dad, did you ever meet him?"

"He was a great guy, but he had a gambling problem. I had to cover a couple bad checks after he lost his job. Right before Christmas 1938, he packed up his stuff and none of us have seen or heard from him since. Your Uncle John may have more information, but that's all I can tell you."

Denny sighed and took a moment to absorb the information and wondered aloud, "Why am I so lucky?"

"You are almost through the worst of it. Stay out of trouble and once you're old enough, you should go into the military. Hopefully, this Korea thing will blow over by then and you can go in during a conflict-free time. Just serve a couple years, then *Uncle Sam* will pay for your college."

"I can see how that would be a good option, but I have a long way to go before I'm at that point."

"I will deny this, but you are my favorite, my first grandchild. You are a smart kid; how could you not be with me as your grandpa and our shared birthday? It may be tough right now, I went through some real hard times as a kid, but I made it through."

"What happened?" asked Denny.

"I don't think I ever told you, but I never spent much time with my dad. When I was two years old, he was working out in the fields and a bull gored him to death. This was in 1882 and he died before a doctor was able to come to the farm and help him. My mother, your great grandmother, eventually remarried, but we had some difficult years after my dad died."

Denny had never heard this story, but he could see how he and his grandpa were similar, never getting to know their fathers. Denny replied, "Sorry that happened to you, I didn't know that."

"It was so long ago now, I have had other heartaches, like when your grandma died. I have won and lost fortunes, but through it all, I have been surrounded by my family and in reflection, I have lived a great life and it's far from over, I still feel fairly young for being 71! His grandpa hugged him, and it felt really nice. Denny cherished these moments of contact and bonding with his family. He would linger a little longer after a hug to imprint these memories for future recall.

Chuck was handing out drinks and hors d'oeuvres, which consisted of deviled eggs and stuffed mushrooms which were tasty.

Fran had definitely spruced up Chuck's 'bachelor pad.' Her little touches were everywhere. The tree was probably the most magnificent addition. It was perfectly shaped, green with white doves and white bows. The two colors together were striking. The presents under the tree were wrapped so meticulously, he was sure that opening one would be a crime.

It was right before dinner when Margo called to say Merry Christmas. Denny already told Chuck if she called, he didn't want to talk to her, which he honored. She was still living in Long Beach and boasted she was having a great Christmas. She didn't even bother to ask if Denny was at Chuck's.

This got Denny thinking, 'Does she even wonder where I am or what I am doing? I must be nothing but an inconvenience to her.' Margo's dad and siblings thought more about Denny than his own mother, and he found this to be despicable and he was disgusted with her. She didn't have a motherly bone in her body. Denny was deep in thought and self-pity when his Uncle Chuck called everyone together for dinner. His family wasn't religious, so no grace was said, but Chuck made a little speech about how it was wonderful to be gathered during the Christmas season and how great it was to have more of the Michigan transplants out in California enjoying summer temperatures in December.

Dinner was wonderful. They ate ham that was glazed in oranges and honey, wonderful baked swirly potatoes, green beans, and some of the softest dinner rolls he had ever eaten.

Denny tried to exercise self-control and not pig out, but the rolls were hard to resist. After practicing self-control, he finally gave in and ate two more after he made sure everyone was finished. Denny had a thing for warm rolls, butter and how they melted in his mouth and warmed his tummy.

After dinner, everyone sat in the living room, talked, and opened presents. Denny hadn't brought much, just some flowers for Fran, that he picked from Billy's house after getting his mom's approval, and a couple of Christmas cards. His family gave him $10 in a card, which was a great surprise for Denny. It made him happy that they were thinking about him, and he was glad he'd dressed up and showered for the occasion. He put on his suit coat, the one he scavenged from the trash and had paired it with a dress shirt and tie he had purchased the week before. His pants were the same pair he brought out from Michigan. Denny's go-to outfits these days were one of two pairs of Levi's and his t-shirts.

It had been nice to see how the other half was living. It was lonely sleeping in the gas station in his tiny room. At least now he was going to school. He liked the social aspect, and he had his crew to pal around with, but overall life was cold and sparse. Nothing compared to Chuck's life.

Denny didn't want to leave, but he didn't want to overstay his welcome. After saying his goodbyes, he rode his bike back into his meager existence, hoping for something better in the future.

Chapter 20

Moving Around Some More

Winter turned to spring, and Denny no longer lived at the gas station, but instead lived out of a carport off Cottage Drive at his buddy Terry Lemere's house. Getting used to Southern California was easy and he noted that the weather was basically the same all the time. Sure, it got cold at night, but it was nothing he couldn't handle. All of his friend's parents had become acquainted with Denny and liked him. On cold nights they would allow him to stay inside if the weather was really bad.

Denny still worked with Fred, but now he was doing more mechanical work, such as repairing flat tires, changing oil, or general clean up at the station. Since he wasn't living in the back of the station anymore, he was making 65 cents an hour, and when he was patching tires or changing them, he earned an extra ten cents for each one.

On Sunday, May 1, 1953, the crew was sitting in the carport playing cards and shooting the shit. All of a sudden, the ground sounded like it popped and then started shaking. Stuff in the carport that was on shelves started to fall. All the boys got up and ran out to the driveway. Denny was right behind them. The ground rumbled for another 20 seconds and then it stopped. They weren't the only ones in the driveway; the rest of Terry's family had run outside as well.

Denny walked to the end of the drive with everyone else. It was dusk outside, but still light out as the sunset. He noticed that all the other neighbors were outside as well and talking about what happened. It was kind of like a neighborhood earthquake party for a while. This was different from the last earthquake because he had people to share it with right after it happened. Being alone last time and not knowing what was happening had been frightening. This time people were standing in the middle of the street talking. Everyone stayed out for about 20 minutes comparing how many pictures fell off the wall or the number of knick-knacks that were broken after falling off shelves. After a bit, they said their goodnights and filtered back to their homes.

It was neat to hear people talking and gathering over a common experience, but it was weird that it took an earthquake for this to happen. Of course, Mr. LeMere knew his neighbors, but Denny hadn't seen this many people in the neighborhood all together; it was cool and weird at the same time. Shit like this didn't happen in Michigan when there was a blizzard, everyone just stayed inside their heated houses trying to stay warm.

That night, Terry had asked his mom if he could stay with Denny and sleep outside, which she agreed to. The boys talked about school, girls, and movies they wanted to watch.

When the boys went to school on Monday, they were presented with three consecutive unsolicited earthquakes. As soon as they walked on campus an earthquake hit, not as big as the one on Sunday, but was still disconcerting to Denny. Once he arrived in his homeroom class the buildings shook again. The pupils were instructed to 'duck and cover' under their desks, when the third aftershock hit. After five minutes they were able to crawl out and finally start class.

For the rest of homeroom class, the students and their teacher talked about earthquakes, what made them happen, the best practices for safety and they had a question-and-answer session. It was a relief not to have a typical class that day, as everyone's nerves were on edge. One question the teacher asked the class was how many kids were not born in California. Out of 30 kids, almost everyone raised their hand. Only five kids were California natives. This was a big surprise to Denny. Much of the discussion focused on the different reactions the students had when an earthquake happened. This made Denny feel better. While he was not a joiner, he was happy to be included in the 'out of towners club.'

Denny was extremely tired at the end of the day. Maybe it was the excitement of the earthquakes or life in general, but he was dog-tired and was going to crash out early. He slept a deep sleep and was thankfully unaware of the turn his life would take the next day.

PART III
MARGO BLOWS
INTO TOWN

Chapter 21

New Dad

Denny felt like he was drowning again. A green 1947 Buick Super convertible had pulled into the pumps. The driver tilted her sunglasses down a bit looked at him and said, "Fill'er up please."

He thought he recognized the woman who sashayed out of the car. She was immaculately dressed in a dark suit, with dark sunglasses and her reddish-brown hair perfectly coiffed. Standing in from of him was the queen bitch herself, his mother, Myrtle Marguerite May, also known as Margo.

A man came around the back of the vehicle where Denny was pumping gas and his mom said, "Denny, I'd like to introduce you to Eugene (Bjarne) Halverson, your stepfather. I call him my Norwegian cowboy."

Denny always stood next to her 'friends' so he could make a size comparison and to see if he could take them in a fight. Father of the year was taller than Denny, he was guessing around six feet three inches in height.

Somehow his mom figured out he was working at the gas station and showed up out of the blue. Last he heard she was living in Long Beach with some chick.

Denny extended his hand to Eugene and said, "Pleased to meet you?"

The news that had his head spinning was what she said next, "We just moved to a house on E Street, up about one block. After you're off work, you should pop by for dinner."

Denny thought, 'are you fucking kidding me right now?'

"Okay, I won't be off until eight tonight, so if you can wait till then it's a date."

Denny was already calculating in his head that he would pop by for a few minutes, then leave. She wanted something from him, and the only way Denny would find out was to visit Margo and see what kind of bullshit would come out of her mouth after the usual exchange of pleasantries. He figured it would be ten minutes before her true intentions became known and then he would formulate his response.

Once he said he would be there, they took off. They waved, he waved, and then poof, she was gone, the same as hundreds of times before.

Since Denny had implemented the 'no contact with Margo' policy and she had not talked to him for over a year, he had a feeling she would be coming for him, if only to renew her status as a mother. She always made a big show of his

birthday, more for herself than him and since she was robbed
of that last year, he had known she was going to make it a
point to be in his face. All of this wasn't for him, it was for
her. Now that she had a new husband, she would want to set
up house for a bit and pretend she was an attentive mother to
him. For his birthdays, the gifts she gave were never useful.
'What would she get me this year? What kind of present do
you give your son who has run away from your ex-husband's
house?'

Before Denny went to military school, he thought his mom
wasn't all bad. As a young boy, he still had hope that she
might be a good mother to him. She still had a chance at
salvation. As Denny became more aware of her escapades and
how other parents behaved, he realized there was no hope of
her becoming the type of mother or woman he could respect.
There had been so many 'husbands' or boyfriends that even
he had lost count of how many there had been.

Fred came over and said, "Who's the doll?"

"That's the woman who gave birth to me."

"The way you talk about your mom, I would have thought
she was the devil herself. She looks like a movie star. Who's
the fella she's with?"

"I guess that's my new dad, which is news to me. Guess
what? You folks are neighbors, she's living around 41st and
E Street and you are at about 46th and E. I am supposed to see
her tonight, for God knows what."

"Are you going to move in with her now that she has relocated here? It might be good to be off the street and eat three square meals a day."

"I'm not sure if that's what I want, I'm getting used to being on my own and at least I'm not being played, like a pawn. Margo is a real puppet master and until you've been around someone like that on a regular basis you won't have any idea what I am talking about. I don't have the energy for it. I am lucky she doesn't know me enough to figure out how to manipulate me, but I have watched it firsthand with Bob and I don't want any part of it."

Fred nodded his head as if he understood the situation and told Denny he knew it was a shock to see his mother and he should knock off early, and he would pay him till the end of his shift. Denny thanked him and took him up on his offer.

As Denny was biking over to the carport to freshen up before he went to his mom's house, he was thinking about the mixed emotions he was feeling about seeing her. Terry's mom, Minnie, said he could get ready in their bathroom, she was always so caring, and he told her how much he appreciated it. During the summer he had been hosing off in the yard, using soap to get clean, so this was a treat. The other way he stayed clean was to use the shower at the Plunge, but nothing compared to a hot shower at the end of the day.

Denny took a deep breath and steeled himself for the visit with his mom. Margo had done well for herself. The place they were renting was a step up from her usual apartments. The house came with a large, fenced yard. He knocked on the door jamb as the screen door was open. Margo told him to come right in. Her husband, Eugene, was lounging in the living room, smoking and she was in the kitchen 'cooking.' Margo wasn't a homemaker, so he wasn't really sure what she was making. It turned out to be chili and cheese over cornbread, which was admirable.

They all sat at the table and made transient conversation that was of no significance. Eugene seemed okay, but Denny wasn't interested in being friends with the flavor of the year. His mom was enamored with him and the way she fawned over him was disgusting.

Denny asked his mom, "So what brings you here?

"I came here for you Denny. I want to provide some stability for my son. When we rented this house, I made sure we had an extra bedroom for my boy. I'd like it if you moved in with us."

'There it was.' He thought, 'why start being concerned for my welfare now?'

"I will need to think about this. I have been living on my own for over a year now, and I feel like I can make a go of it. It's been hard, but not horrible. I have a group of friends I go to school with, and their parents help me out sometimes. I have a job and I'm doing okay."

"You can't live on your own, you are a minor and you need to come and live with me!"

Denny sensed storm clouds were gathering and he was preparing for the rain and thunder. This was his cue to leave. His mom didn't know where he was staying, and he was going to keep it that way. He wormed his hand away from hers, stood up, gave her a hug, thanked her and Eugene for dinner and headed out the front door.

Denny yelled, "I'll come around next week, and we can do dinner again."

Denny got on his bike and jetted around the corner super quick to lose anyone who might be following him and headed back to the carport. A long time ago he learned the best thing to do was to leave, instead of sticking around fighting with Margo. He had witnessed too many arguments where his mom would switch back and forth, at will, between psycho bitch and saint. She would yell, scream, throw a tantrum with her demands, and then like walking into a room for the first time, she would be sweet as pie. Margo would get this look on her face that was like a smile, a smirk, with a helping of bitch thrown in all-in-one. When Denny saw this expression, he knew it was time to leave her the fuck alone. If he didn't, she would start throwing things, but the worst part would be the words she would speak. Her words would cut through him and damage his soul. Margo's words could never be unheard or taken back. Instead, he would run away rather than suffer her wrath.

By the time Denny found his buddy Terry, his heart had slowed its racing, and they hung out talking. Terry's family was nice; he had an older brother and sister. Terry was the youngest in the family.

Terry was cool, just a year younger than Denny. Terry asked, "Did you know your mom was in town? What kind of shit is that to surprise you at work? I don't understand it."

"It's some fucked up kind of shit, that's what it is. I wish she hadn't shown up right now, I was on track to a great summer. The only thing that is going to save me is that she is currently working at the Skadron school of business, so she will be busy during the day. As for her Norwegian cowboy, I am not sure what his deal is, but he has no hold over me and if he thinks he can pull a fast one on me, he'll find out soon enough I'm no pushover."

"Yep, this has a possibly of messing up our whole summer."

Sometimes at night, during the summer, Terry would hang out with him. This was one of those nights, they just hung out lying on camping cots in the car port and planning the rest of their summer without Margo.

Chapter 22

Rough Day

"Dammit Denny!" Margo was having a bit of a tantrum at Eugene's expense.

Eugene tried to soothe her in his stilted accent, "Perhaps it's better if he doesn't live here. I understand you wanted to try and set up a home for him, but if he wants to stay out on his own, maybe you should let him."

Since Denny left, Margo had been going on and on about Denny, saying things like, "After all I have done for him, this is how he treats me! He is an ungrateful shit. Somedays I wish he was never born. He thoroughly fucked up my life for his first five years. I had to find places for him to stay while I was working to provide for him." She went on ad nauseam about how many inconveniences Denny created in her life by being born.

Margo was also smoking non-stop for about two hours and was on her third drink. The next thing she remembered was waking up with a start at 3am. Eugene was asleep in his chair, so Margo got up and went to bed. She knew this school day was going to be rough, so she popped a couple aspirin before turning in.

Waking up was always hard. The first thing Margo did before she did anything else in the morning was smoke a Phillip Morris, king-size cigarette. Above anything else, in the morning, the cigarette came first, then Alka-Seltzer. Margo was on her second cigarette before she got up.

School started at 9am, so Margo got up around 7:30am to get ready. It was a short, ten-minute drive to work. She worked at Skadron College down on 7th Street in San Bernardino and was the main teacher for stenography, spelling, and word usage. She was also the Faculty Social Director. One thing she took pride in was her appearance and she always dressed to impress. That particular day was going to be a challenge, though. Her hair stank like cigarettes, which usually she didn't notice, but it was particularly pungent, and her breath smelled like she had eaten a pint of gin instead of only drinking it.

Eugene had already gone to work at the machine shop when Margo got up. Margo didn't have time to do much with her appearance, so she got up, took a shower, and started the process of her daily routine.

She styled her hair around a white silk scarf and sprayed perfume on it to mask the stench of stale cigarettes. She went to the salon and got her hair shampooed and set once a week. Margo usually slept with rollers in her hair and toilet paper covering her set, so it didn't get messed up. Since none of that happened the previous night and because her hair was thick, almost unmanageable, she decided to cover the mess with a scarf. She was going to see if she could go in earlier than her next appointment to freshen her hair up.

Since it was summer, Margo picked a sleeveless white top, with a navy skirt and jacket combo. She would take her coat off when she was outside in the summer heat. She packed lunch but wasn't sure how she would feel about eating it later. Nothing fancy, just peanut butter, and bread.

By the time she got to work she'd smoked two more cigarettes and cursed Denny a half-dozen more times. When she pulled up at the curb, she put on her trademark orangish red lipstick and was ready to face the day.

She had three classes to teach, one from 9am-11am, lunch, and two more classes from 1pm-3pm and 3pm-5pm. One day a week she stayed late and taught a class from 6-7pm, and praise Jesus, that was not that particular night. This last class was mainly about office etiquette and decorum.

Mostly all of Margo's students were really just girls trying to become women in a man's world. They would mainly be taking dictation, typing letters, making sure the letters made sense and most important of all, making the boss look competent and professional.

High on the list of things to teach these secretaries in training was to conduct themselves in a manner that was beyond reproach by others and to never ever let their guard down. If they were going to be part of a secretarial pool in an office, the goal was to work your way up to be a dedicated secretary to one man. This was where the financial and personal gains became more lucrative. This environment could be cut-throat, and competition was high for the one-on-one secretarial positions.

Margo also taught the girls about practicing discretion regarding anything overheard in 'the boss's office.' This ran the gamut from business deals he's working on to how he was thinking about divorcing his wife. This all needed to be 'hush hush.' She realized there was very little room for advancement beyond these positions, but a secretary could make decent money if she made herself invaluable.

She wasn't sure how many of her students would eventually become the boss's wife, but she was fairly sure that most of them were aiming for marriage instead of being typing pool secretaries. Possibly a few of them would become bookkeepers and take off with the company fortune. Instructors never had great insight into their students motivations or who they were training. If Margo had an office job, her aspirations would be to grab everything she could, there was no moral high ground for her, and she would have no regrets about taking advantage of every opportunity placed within her grasp.

Margo met Eugene when she was living in Long Beach and was immediately enamored with him. She loved his height, accent, and personality. They met on the beach and were married within six weeks.

Margo was the queen of exiting a relationship. She made her plans and packed while Jeanna was at work and waited for a day when Jeanna had to take care of something at her daughter's school. The trick was to leave enough things around the house so no notice was taken of items being packed or secreted away in a suitcase, in the trunk of a car.

On the day of 'the leaving' Margo threw the rest of her clothes and shoes in the trunk haphazardly, grabbed the dog, hastily wrote a goodbye note, and left some cash on the table to help with the next month's rent and bills. After all she wasn't heartless. Margo and Eugene had already been married for a week at this point, so she justified her actions: because she was a married woman, she must leave.

Part of her exit plan included taking a trip out to San Bernardino where she applied for a job with Skadron Business College. This position was more of a year-round position, with only minimal breaks for summer and holidays. Eugene was staying at a cousin's house, and she was able to stay with him a couple weeks until they could move into the house in San Bernardino, close to her boy, but more importantly close to her brothers Chuck and Milt and her 'daddie.' A girl never could tell when she might need some additional support.

Margo didn't revisit her past relationships and she wasn't going to start doing so with Jeanna. She always faced forward. The only time she glanced back was to remind people in her life what she had done for them or search for a way to make them feel guilty about a perceived past wrong. Money was the other carrot that would turn her head toward the past, like her situation with Bob. Margo was in it for Margo and nobody else.

Looking forward, it was a little painful in that her bid to have Denny come live with her had not worked but she would keep wheedling and whining her way in. Margo was convinced eventually she would win him over. The carrot here was to boost her self-esteem and to be able to tell herself and show to her family that she was a good mom.

Margo got along well with Mr. Skadron, the president and owner of the college, as well as her co-workers, but kept things strictly business as this job was extremely important to her as she was making fair money for 1953, almost $5,000 a year. She took over from another teacher who had a baby and would be staying at home to become a house mouse. This meant Margo would be a full-time employee, which was exactly what she wanted.

None of her coworkers had any hint of her struggles with her son, and she was going to keep it that way. She would only talk about him in the loosest terms. The other thing that she kept private was how many times she had been married and divorced; she was on number four. She also didn't tell people her real age; this included her husbands. She found out a while ago, while they do ask for identification at the time you apply for a marriage license, they let you put your birthdate in the register, and it wasn't unheard of for her to shave off five to seven years depending on how laxed the county clerk was with the registration. It was kind of a game to her, and if the wrong date was discovered, she glossed it over. She only got caught once and she said, "Oh, let me fix that, sometimes my writing isn't very clear, I am a shorthand teacher, and I am forever putting things in shorthand instead of normal cursive." But Margo knew different.

Chapter 23

California Snow

Most of the summer of 1953 was Margo-free. Denny asked Fred for his birthday off, which didn't go the way he planned. The day before was crazy. He had never witnessed a forest fire like the one that day and on his birthday. A fire started above the Arrowhead Landmark and threatened the Arrowhead Springs Hotel. After he got off work, he and his buddies biked over to the top of Sierra Way and watched the fire.

Denny had never seen anything like it, yet people who were watching the fire with them said it was a fairly frequent occurrence. To Denny this was a weird community event, similar to when the earthquake happened, but instead they were watching a fire. One firewatcher said, "We are super lucky that the Santa Anas aren't blowing."

Denny asked, "What's a Santa Ana?"

The man told him, "Those are scary high winds that can almost knock a grown man down. They come through in the fall and early spring and are crazy strong. We have fires like this a couple times a year, why hell, the hotel itself has been burned to the ground two or three times!"

Denny marveled how this was an acceptable part of living in this area. It was such a strange remark as if to say, 'Yeah, the hills burn occasionally and that's okay, business as usual.'

It was chaotic with all of the fire engine trucks heading 'up the hill' and firemen staged at different areas. The bitter smoke filled the air and ash rained from the sky. Denny guessed this was probably the only kind of snow San Bernardino ever got and was not the kind anybody wanted.

The boys headed to the area south of the flood control dike above 40th Street. As Denny surveyed his surroundings, it appeared all the residents of the North End had come out to watch the fire. Since it was summer, the boys biked around to different vantage points to watch it. They also went over to the east Twin Creek Wash which was to the east of the hotel to check it out.

Denny wasn't able to see much, and he certainly couldn't make out the Arrowhead Landmark. Flames leaped into the air illuminating the white façade of the hotel. Denny had questioned quite a few people about the Arrowhead, and he learned it was made up of scrub bushes and flat rocks. The locals were convinced it was a natural occurrence, however, over the years they had shored it up with plantings and other various techniques were employed to ensure it remained visible for generations to come.

Some people said the hot springs were sacred Indian grounds and that the Arrowhead Landmark pointed to the springs. Denny wanted to know more, so while they were cruising around, he would ask some of the older people about the hotel. Three hotels had been built on this site previously: one was a homestead, the second one was built in the early 1800s, and the third one was built by a famous architect, by the last name of Benton, but that one burnt down too. This last hotel was built in the 1930s and was used as a Naval Convalescent Hospital during World War II.

Recently the Hilton corporation purchased the property, remodeled it, built a new pool, shaped like an arrowhead, and had only re-opened it a couple of months before. Everyone agreed it would be a tragedy if it burned for a fourth time. If the hotel survived Denny was going to make it a point to visit the grounds and check it out. It was said that famous people visited the hotel and Denny wanted to add his name to that list.

The boys stayed up till about midnight, when they called it a night and headed back home. The fire took on a completely different appearance at night as the boys watched the bright orange flames leap into the night sky against the darkened hills. It was terrifying and spellbinding at the same time. The moon was almost full and that night, at times it was a reddish pink due to all the smoke and ash in the air. As they rode back to their houses, Denny suspected there was smoke in his lungs making him cough. It was going to be hard sleeping outside tonight; he was going to cover his head to keep the ash out.

When Denny woke up the next day, he was congested and boogery. When he pushed his sleeping bag off to stand up, ashes scattered everywhere. Some ashes were a half an inch in size and were gray striped with black. The size and variation of the ashes was a surprise to him. As Denny walked around, the ashes fluttered around with each step, and it continued to snow from the sky. He must have blown his nose a dozen times before his nose and throat were clear of the ash. Denny thought, 'Well, happy fifteenth birthday to me.'

That day he cruised around town with his buddies. Jim, Terry, and Billy offered to take him out to breakfast at a little coffee shop.

The place was full of people talking about the fire and how the firefighters were able stop the fire in time to save the hotel. *The San Bernardino Sun* had a detailed newspaper article about the fire and Denny was surprised to hear there had been three other fires the day before, which gave him pause. It made him wonder if someone intentionally started these fires, some sicko psycho who should be at Patton State Hospital instead of roaming free starting fires. His breakfast was so huge he figured it would hold him until he went to his mom's house for a 'special dinner' that night.

Denny and his crew went riding around again like they did the day before. The fire was more under control and dying down. It had moved into other canyons, some over by the Del Rosa area of town.

After a full day of messing around, Denny grabbed some clothes and went over to his mom's house. Eugene was home so Denny asked if he could use the shower before dinner to wash the soot and ash off. Eugene agreed and Denny spent a full 20 minutes in the shower, he plugged the drain with his feet, so he was able to see much grime he was washing off. When the water ran clear, he would be clean. Since living on his own, he had come to appreciate the little things like taking a shower.

While he was taking care of his hygiene, Margo came home and was starting Denny's new favorite meal, tacos. Before he moved out to California, he had never been exposed to them, but Mexican food was now his 'go to' food. His mom actually did a good job with tacos, but they were hard to screw up, even for her. They were basically corn tortillas cooked in oil, ground meat, shredded cheddar, tomatoes, onions, lettuce, and jalapeno peppers. Denny also liked to throw in hot sauce. It was a very economical meal. His mom had made extra meat at Denny's request because he would easily put away six to ten tacos on his own. Any leftovers may be a meal for Eugene and Margo later, but with Denny around that was highly unlikely.

Dinner was actually enjoyable, and his mom was on her best behavior for a change. After dinner they sat in the living room and his mom gave him a gift. It wasn't a gift but more a promise to teach him how to drive a car. This was valuable since he was in driver's ed at school and the next step would be the practice part of driving. The other things she gave him was some underwear and a dop bag to put his toiletries in. She had also made him a small birthday cake complete with candles. Denny made a wish and blew the candles out.

Denny wished for the same thing he always wished for, to be loved by both of his parents. Denny's heart was softening a bit when it came to Margo and asked her and Eugene, "Would it be alright after I am back in school, if I come and live with you? I want to wait until I go back to school because I am enjoying my summer and freedom."

His mom got up, came over and gave him a hug and said, "Of course you can." Denny hung out with Eugene and Margo for a while and watched television; *The Groucho Marx Show* was on. He left around 10pm to head back to the carport.

As Denny fell asleep that night, he thought about what he had committed to and was hoping he wouldn't regret his decision.

Chapter 24

Santa Anas

Summer turned into fall and Denny had his first major experience with strong Santa Anas. Yes, he experienced wind in Detroit, but nothing like these winds. These were hot and super dry. Denny was learning living in Southern California had its advantages, but it was also a weird place, what with the coyotes, wildfires, earthquakes, tumbleweeds, and now the 'devil winds.' This was indeed the wild west.

The first time a tumbleweed rolled and bounced past Denny, he thought it was funny. Tumbleweeds are dried-up sticker bushes that are ball shaped. Every so often, a car would run over one head-on. They would disintegrate. Located across from the gas station was a fence that must have had 50 of these bushes piled up. You didn't want to be close to a tumbleweed because all over these dried-up bushes were thorns that would get stuck in the soles of your shoes, and they were a bitch to pick out. Sometimes they would stick in the cuffs of Denny's jeans. They were sticky, clingy, thorny, and it was best to avoid them at all costs.

At first the wind was entertaining, and Denny was going to try and fly. He had a light jacket on and with his arms still in the sleeves he inverted his jacket over his head and made a sail, like an inverted cape. Then he tried to walk facing the direction of the wind. It was a way to test how strong he was, and he really wasn't making any headway. Crazy how powerful these winds were. Denny thought, 'If I was a little lighter, I might catch air and take off like Superman.'

Fred said that these winds came up off the desert floor and started building velocity once they were funneled into the Cajon Pass. Denny wouldn't doubt it if they were blowing 60mph. Once the winds died down in a couple days, he might go to the airport to see what they had to say about the speed of the winds. Denny had branched out a bit. Lately he had been going to the airport with his buddies. They would watch the pilots flying planes. They even met some of the pilots who kept their planes at the airport. Pilots were super interesting people; they would make small talk with them when they had the time.

The wind was strange. It made his throat itch, and his nose immediately plugged up when they started blowing through town. Maybe his congestion was due to the dirt and all the other crap flying around in the air. Denny didn't really get sick, so this was annoying. His feelings about the wind were mixed. Denny imagined if he was up in the mountains looking over the valley one could probably see the Pacific Ocean. Once the wind was over the skies would crystal clear but not this day. This day, the wind tossed kids' lost homework, teachers' notes, leaves, and the occasional trash can to a new destination.

Denny was careful about pumping gas, otherwise he would get a gas bath. This had already happened once. When filling up cars sometimes the drivers would ask him to check under the hood for water and oil levels. He was extra careful about that too as he didn't need a heavy hood slamming down on him. While making conversation, he told people to be careful when opening and closing their car door. A customer had actually been knocked down to the ground when his car door hit him due to a strong gust of wind. Denny always caught a little break when closing up the station if it was windy. There was no sense sweeping up at night to then do it again in the morning.

Getting to and from school was not fun in the wind. Thank God he bought the Whizzer bike, a motorized bicycle. He got a great deal on it from a lady whose husband wasn't using it anymore on account that she was divorcing him. She was selling it to spite him. The new bike made things a lot easier to get from one place to the next and he really appreciated it on windy days.

Over the summer his mom kept pestering him about moving to her house. At the end of September, he moved in with her and Eugene as a trial. Denny tried not to stick around the house too much, but it was comforting to have a regular bed to sleep in instead of living rough. It was okay when his mom wasn't putting on a show about how caring she was.

His stepdad was a piece of shit, the typical kind of man his mom was attracted to. Eugene had a job, but Denny wasn't sure about what he did for work, and he didn't care. However, Denny recognized he was a drunk. His mom also liked to knock them back. At least Bob wasn't a boozer.

Eugene, as he liked to be called instead of his real name Bjarne, was supposedly a fireman when he was living in San Diego. He was born in Norway, hence the nickname Norwegian cowboy, which was gross. Sometimes he wore a cowboy hat and liked to dress up in western clothes. Denny was sure Eugene's nickname had some type of sexual escapade component that went along with the costume, but as long as he didn't know about it, he didn't care.

A couple of things bugged him about the living situation. Smoking was one of his all-time pet peeves. Denny never smoked; it wasn't his thing. If a girl smoked, she was automatically crossed off his available list. His aversion to cigarettes was because his mom was a chain smoker. When she wasn't working, she was smoking, and Eugene was the same way. Ashes were everywhere, and it was a constant thing that needed to be cleaned up.

Denny's experience with his mom's smoking was that she did it to avoid work or real conversations. If she had a cigarette, her hands were always busy and that meant she was busy too. It was a stall tactic to drag time out so she could act like she forgot what was being asked of her. She'd say "Hey, let me finish this cigarette before we do whatever it is you want me to do." Or, "Hey, before we go, I'm gonna grab a smoke, be back in a flash." After about 20 minutes, she was still smoking in hopes that the person who was hassling her would just give up. Surprisingly, the house was clean. Eugene did the majority of the cleaning with Denny pitching in to take out the trash and perform various other chores.

The other thing that bugged Denny was his mom's dog. Margo called him Jackie because he was a Jack Russell Terrier. Denny didn't have a problem with the dog or dogs in general, he had an issue with what the dog represented to him. Apparently, his mom owned this dog for the past three years and took care of him very well, fed him, bathed him, housed him, and took him to the vet when needed.

The dog was a constant companion. She did more for this dog than she did for her own son. At first Denny thought the dog was Eugene's, but after a bit he figured out his mom got the dog when she was living in Long Beach. There was quite a big fuss about her taking the dog when she left. Jeanna's little girls had grown attached to him and they considered the dog as much theirs as Margo's, but being the selfish bitch that she was, she took the dog with her upon her abrupt exit. Denny liked the dog enough and was kind to it, but the fact that his mom took better care of a dog than her own child was indefensible.

Denny tried not to ask for favors from either Margo or Eugene, otherwise it just became fodder for them to hold over his head when they wanted him to do something. Denny kept hanging out with his friends and chatting up the chicks at school and working. He had met some guys who hung out behind the station in the wash area. These friends helped him a little with questions he had about his Whizzer bike when he needed to fix it. Billy, Jim, and Denny hung out at least one to two nights a week with them. The older guys were cool because they occasionally had girls with them.

The most exciting thing that happened during this time was when his mom's car was stolen. There was a lot of excitement and it turned out to be some kids joy riding. Margo and Eugene were in an uproar for the five days her car was missing. His mom was at work and when she was ready to come home, she walked outside, and her car was gone. Truth be told, she didn't want the car back; what she wanted was an excuse to buy a new car. The car ended up getting totaled and she was extremely happy about that.

Denny was going to hang onto this gig of staying with his mom until it no longer served a purpose for him. The reason he was staying was because winter was coming, and he wanted to be inside during that time. Because San Bernardino was so close to the mountains, the temperature could drop as low as the 28 degrees at night. While this wasn't Detroit cold, it was cold enough that Denny wanted to be inside. The rainy season went through April, and although he had lucked out with the weather the past two years, next year might be a little different.

Chapter 25

Christmas 1953 and the New Boxing Champion

Christmas 1953 was fun as his Uncle John came to visit from Michigan, with his wife, Marian, and stayed at Margo's for about a week. Uncle John was always pleasant and jovial.

One afternoon, they were outside sitting in the yard, soaking up the sun and Denny asked John, "Did you know my dad?"

John said, "Yes, I did, Gene was a good man and extremely charming. He was a salesperson, and he could sell anything to anybody. Unfortunately, he ran into some trouble with the FBI because he was impersonating government employees and writing bad checks." This was the first Denny heard he was impersonating people, but he was all ears while he listened to his uncle.

"Two FBI agents came to visit me in 1949 and said that your mom asked them to re-open the case. Something about your dad's dad dying, he would have been your Grandpa

Dulin. A substantial inheritance was due, and your mom was trying to collect it for you. Since your dad was never declared dead, only missing, she never got the money. The agents told me that they lost track of him during the war but found out later he joined the Royal Canadian Air Force and had flown Spitfires in the Battle of Britain, and after that he joined the French Foreign Legion and died in Algiers in 1949. I am not sure how much of this was true, but that's what they told me. The problem with the French Foreign Legion is that they don't use names and these records would be hard to come by. So, I guess it's a mystery what truly happened to him."

Denny was speechless as this was a large amount of information for his young mind to absorb. He wondered, 'Is my dad dead?' Over the years, he thought about him frequently, but he was always hopeful one day he would come back and help him out. It was news to Denny that his mom had been trying to learn information about his dad to see if she could get the inheritance money. Of course, if there was an inheritance, you could bet she would have kept it for herself and not given Denny any of it. Margo didn't speak about his dad, and it was irritating as Gene, may have been a passing dalliance for her, but he was much more than that to Denny, Gene was his dad. While Margo grew up in a complete and loving home, Denny had none of those things and she didn't have a fucking clue how that made him feel.

There were so many questions he had for John, so it was weird that the first words that popped out his mouth were, "Wow, do you think my dad has an FBI file?"

"I know he does, that's what the agents said."

Denny sat with John talking about his house and where he lived, his son Gary, Denny's cousin, and life in general. John recognized that Denny had gotten a raw deal with Myrt as his mom and told him once he got a little older and was out of school, he was welcome to spend some time with him back in Michigan, if he wanted to. John did acknowledge that California would be a hard act to follow weather-wise.

It took Denny a while to process what John told him. During the Christmas break, Denny could be found hanging out with his crew or working. Christmas fell on a Friday, which meant no work on Thursday or Friday, so he was able to relax during this time.

On Christmas day, they all met at Chuck and Fran's new house. His mom's other brother Milt and family came as well, and his Grandpa May who was there with his wife Hazel. It was great to be together with family. His Aunt Babe and family were living in Oregon and his Aunt Ruthie, and her family were absent as well.

Margo was on her best behavior, as was Eugene. Denny dressed up in a button-down shirt and khakis his mom bought him. Denny came over on his own so he could leave when he wanted to. His Uncle Chuck's new house was beautiful.

Chuck and Fran had bought a house on Broadmoor over by the golf course and it was only a year old.

This gathering gave Denny a false sense of belonging and a glimpse of how life might have been for him, if his mom was a normal mom. Oh, how he longed for this, but it was bittersweet because it was something unattainable. Directly off the entry a beautiful Christmas tree was displayed which was brightly lit with bubble lights. This time the tree was multicolored but still classy, and the house was perfect.

A lovely meal of prime rib was served, complete with Christmas pudding. Fran and Chuck were gracious hosts. It was a perfect day. San Bernardino had been through a major bout of Santa Ana winds for the past two days which stopped right before Christmas day providing a beautiful bright day as a backdrop.

It was funny to watch her interact with her family. His mom always went by Margo, but grandpa always called her Myrt, as did her other siblings. Seeing his grandpa again was great, but the way his mom behaved around him was odd. His mom called her father, 'daddie,' which was so weird because she was a grown ass woman.

Her behavior showed she had never really did grow up. Observing Margo these past few months confirmed Denny's beliefs that she was selfish and immature. Margo's predictable move when challenged or things weren't going her way was to tell someone to go to hell.

If she happened to be talking on the phone, she would slam the receiver down so hard the bell in the base of the phone would chime. Ending a phone call this way required dexterity. This skill involved holding the receiver a certain way, so fingers didn't get smashed between the handset and the base in the heat of the hang up. The satisfaction she received from a brisk hangup would be magnified if she had an audience. After seeing this happen a couple of times, it had lost the desired effect on Denny and became more comical to him than she ever intended.

His observations of his mom's behavior were practically clinical. Taking mental notes of these antics would no doubt serve him well in the future. Denny's beliefs that she was selfish, and immature had been validated multiple times over these past few months he had been living with her, which had been the most time he ever spent with his mom.

Being with the family was enjoyable that week, but then it was back to reality, back to school, and back to survival mode.

In February 1954, things started to unravel on the home front. It was a Saturday evening and Denny was working on his Whizzer, cleaning it up from performing an oil change and washing it. Eugene came out and asked if it would be okay if he took his Whizzer for a spin. Denny graciously let him ride it.

Eugene didn't come back for about two hours, which was a total dick move. When he did come back, he was hammered. Denny let this go, but he was pissed because he had planned on going to 'the spot' with the boys. Denny was sure his crew would still be at the wash, and he could catch up with them, but taking off for so long with his bicycle was inconsiderate at the very least. Denny was going to speak with him the next day about this incident.

When Denny caught up with his friends partying in the arroyo, they added fuel to Denny's fiery anger as it simmered regarding Eugene. Denny didn't get along with him from the beginning, but now he was going to put him in his place. Margo said Eugene used to be a boxer, supposedly the champion of Norway boxing in 1941, so he got a few pointers from the guys in case things got out of hand.

The guys didn't tell Denny anything he didn't already know. His fighting days in Detroit taught him more than any of the tips he received. From what they were telling him, he doubted if they had fought in many fights. Denny had gotten the shit beaten out of him and he had done his fair share of beating the shit out of his bullies. He also had a backup plan to have all of his gear packed and ready if he had to split and stay at Jim's place. Jim's parents were cool, and he would be able to crash there for a while.

The next morning, Eugene and his mom were hungover and drinking Bloody Marys, so this was the perfect time to ask Eugene about the Whizzer. Denny put his bag on the back of his bike and was ready to head out if needed.

As they sat in the dining area Denny said, "Eugene, I would appreciate it if you are going to borrow my stuff that you would tell me how long you are going to be using it. I had plans last night and didn't expect that you would take my bike out for two hours."

Eugene replied, "That's not your bike, that's my bike, and I will take it out for as long as I want to."

"I have the pink on that bike, it's mine!"

Denny made a beeline for the front door and walked outside.

Eugene followed him and stood in front of his bike, nose to nose with Denny.

Denny, yelled right in Eugene's face, "This is my motherfucking bike, not yours, I paid for this bike, fuck you, Norwegian cowboy!"

Margo ran after both of them. Caterwauling as she was running, "Stop! Stop, both of you!"

Eugene backed up and made a fist as if he was going to hit Denny, and sternly shouted, "Are you threatening me boy?"

"No, threat here."

Denny punched him directly in the nose. Eugene dropped to his knees and his mom rushed to her husband. Denny hopped on his bike.

As he was leaving, he said, "Sorry, I can't live with this guy!"

Chapter 26

Arrowhead Springs

Denny's adrenaline was pumping as he took off from his mom's house. He was going to take a long ride somewhere along the foothills to clear his head. The road he drove was directly below and parallel to the foothills and headed east. It was windy, and it reminded him of summer when his mom blew into town with that asshole husband of hers. It was hard not to draw comparisons between sudden shifts in the weather and his tumultuous relationship with his mother.

As Denny wound around the foothills, he guided his bike along the path next to the raised bed of the old Pacific Electric Railway tracks, that were used by the 'water train.' This train ran along the old tracks and brought water from Arrowhead Springs to the Arrowhead and Puritas company in San Bernardino. The train didn't run on the weekend, so Denny followed the path to the Arrowhead Springs Hotel. Quite a brouhaha was made about these tracks and the citizens were trying to stop the water train. It was kind of an eyesore; it ran right through the middle of town.

As he drove, he tried to think about other things not related to Margo, so he started musing about the foothills. 'As in, why are they called foothills?' Denny understood that they were likely called foothills because they were at the base or foot of the mountain, but Denny thought the little hills looked like actual feet. Some had four toes, others had six. But if you examined them, they began to resemble the toes on a foot. He pondered this for a little longer as he rode and concluded that was exactly why they were called foothills.

Some slang terms were used when the locals spoke about the mountains. They would say I'm going, 'up the hill' or I just came 'down the hill,' this might refer to Crestline or anywhere in the local mountains or the high desert including 'the pass.' The Cajon Pass led up to the high desert and would sometimes be differentiated by people saying they were headed 'up the pass' or 'down the pass,' but not always, so that was a little confusing.

These were some of the things he hadn't heard anywhere else. When customers who lived 'up the hill' would stop for gas, especially if the weather was bad, they would complain about how they hoped no 'flatlanders' were going to try and go 'up the hill,' because they didn't know how to drive and were always causing accidents.

These random thoughts kept Denny's mind occupied as he crossed the road and drove over to the entrance of the Arrowhead Springs Hotel. At the head of the driveway that led to the front of the hotel, a Native American statue stood that was pointing to the hot springs and the hotel. Denny continued to ride his motorbike along the road until he found a spot to park. He was dressed well, and he felt like he could blend in as someone's kid.

Walking into the lobby made him feel like an imposter. Denny shook the feeling off and absorbed the ambience of the hotel, which was magnificent. There was a full set of windows that curved out and provided a view of the pool. Denny sat in one of the chairs in the nicely furnished lobby and imagined what it would be like to stay at this hotel. All of the women at the hotel were elegantly dressed. It made Denny wonder if they were planning on going to church that morning. The pool was open, but due to the early hour, no one was swimming. It was a little cold, so there would be no bathing suit action.

After a while of rich people watching, Denny wandered outside to the pool area and sat in one of the chairs. He thought, 'Who designed this place?' From what he understood, this rendition of the hotel had been built around 1940. The one constant for this area were the hot springs and having a hotel at that spot.

Denny was admiring the grounds when he spotted the burn marks on the hill behind the hotel. 'Damn, the fire had been really close to the building.' Denny wandered around a little bit more and found the hot springs. They were located in a cave-like place. Someday he might come back when he was feeling more adventurous. It might be kind of fun to put on airs and walk around; he had never hung out at a luxurious hotel before. He could be a phantom kid of one of the guests.

This little trip had taken him out of his own head and put his attitude back where it needed to be for an encounter with Jim's parents.

Denny figured, if the Christie family went to church, they would already be home and starting to relax for a possible early Sunday afternoon meal or a lazy nap. Although Jim and Denny already worked things out with Jim's parents, Denny wanted to confirm everything with them one more time. They owned a 3-bedroom house, but there was only one bathroom for six people. They also kept two horses in the back of the house, which was fine; he had been around horses before with his Grandpa May.

His grandpa raised and trained horses called Tennessee Walkers back in Michigan. Denny was going to be living in the detached garage in the back. He would pay $2.50 a week or $10 a month to live there and was able use the shower when Jim's dad got home from work. The garage was much nicer than the carport he lived in previously, but definitely a step below living with his mom and Eugene; at least he didn't need to put up with their crap anymore.

The Christies were a friendly family. Denny wasn't sure what Mr. Christie did for a living, but he thought he worked at the Arrowhead Country Club playing golf, which sounded like a fun job to Denny. Mrs. Christie liked to play the piano. Music was always playing at the house and in general everyone was happy. Leah, Jim's sister, broke her leg in a horse-riding accident the previous year, but had fully recovered. The two younger kids, Sally and Ricky were always underfoot, but good kids.

The best thing for Denny was that all of his friends lived fairly close together and all in the North End of San Bernardino. It never took him more than five minutes to go to anyone's house or even his job. Denny also enjoyed the camaraderie of being part of a group and feeling accepted. Because Denny moved so often when he was with his mom, being on his own in some strange way offered him stability in his relationships with others which he previously had no control over. At least here, he was able to stay for a while and form some bonds with kids his own age.

Denny was now going to San Bernardino High School, which was even farther than Arrowview Junior High. The trip wasn't too bad now that he had his motorized bike. Riding his pedal bike over the foothills had been a ball buster.

The best thing about San Bernardino High School was a place called McDonald's a couple of blocks down E Street. Denny and his buddies would run over for lunch and get a hamburger for 15 cents. It was a great deal, and the food was super-hot and fresh. The other thing that was super-hot and fresh were all of the girls that also ate lunch there. Not only were kids from his high school around, but so were kids from Colton and Pacific High Schools as well. This was the place to be seen. The kids from those schools told him, if they timed it right, they could make it to McDonald's and back with five minutes to spare.

Lunch time was at its best when Denny was sitting in the parking lot of McDonald's, eating his burger, being cool and checking out girls. This became quite the hangout for him, as well as everyone else, and he could eat cheaply, sometimes a couple times a day.

The other cool thing he learned about from the kids at McDonald's was what they called 'Cruising E Street.' This happened every Friday and Saturday night; it was a continuous teenage party in the streets. They would start at Court Street and E Street and cruise all the way up past McDonald's, then turn around above Highland Avenue and do it again. Some people wouldn't even cruise, they would park their hot rods and sit around talking. Denny didn't have a car to cruise in, so usually, he took his Whizzer. Sure, people would laugh, but not everyone, and at least he was in the middle of the whole wonderful mess.

It was common for everyone to climb in the car, blast their music and scream their phone numbers out over the blaring radio. Guys would beef up their cars with loud pipes and raise the rear end so when they did a burn out it really showed off the smoke. The guys with the hottest cars would cruise with their girlfriends right next to them in the front seat, usually with a pile of miscellaneous friends in the back seat being all crazy.

Denny would occasionally pile in a car with some older kids and ride around. Jim took out his mom's station wagon every once in a while, but for the most part he was solo on these nights; but not always alone at the end of the night.

Denny's grades weren't great. He was earning D's or F's; the only classes he was passing currently were PE, typing, and automotive. English, geometry, Spanish, and even driver's ed were lost causes as he headed into the second part of his sophomore year. It was tough to pay attention especially when he had girls, motorcycles, cruising, and having a good time on his mind.

Chapter 27

Being Cool

As the school year finished up, Denny found he was spending time with his crew and hanging out more with the guys in the wash behind the station. When Denny wasn't there, he frequented the Plunge, was working, or just running around doing stupid stuff.

One night they partied with a dummy. Usually, the guys would each take one to two beers from their parents' refrigerators and bring them out to 'the spot.' This time they took a store mannequin they found in dumpster. The boys named him Joe. They took an empty beer can and posed the dummy drinking it, holding it and the boys had random conversations with the dummy. Joe was having a grand old time until Denny took him for a ride on the back of his Whizzer. Joe bit the dust on Kendall Drive and Denny chose to leave him there.

It was funny when, two days later, the newspaper ran a story about how the cops thought some guy was lying drunk or dead in the road, but when they came up to him, they discovered it wasn't a human at all. The boys got a kick out of describing the event to anyone who would listen. Watching them tell the story was very funny because they would break out in giggles as they struggled to finish telling the tale.

Denny was going to buy an Indian motorcycle for his birthday. An acquaintance had a 'bike in a box' that was available for 50 bucks. This was not a decision he made lightly, as he had to make sure he had a cushion in case of an emergency. Spending all his money on one thing was not an option. Even after buying the bike, he had triple that amount saved for any unplanned expenses. He continued to be frugal and very rarely spent money on non-essential stuff. Every day he wore his leather jacket and aviator sunglasses; these were essential items for being cool. The jacket was 15 bucks, and the glasses were 19 cents, purchased from his favorite army surplus store.

Right after Denny bought the motorcycle, he rushed to the gas station and showed Fred.

"Wow, this thing is going to be a death trap. We'll do the best we can with what we have." Fred took stock of everything in the box and made a list of things they would need. "You can work on this project here when you are off, but not while you are working for me."

Denny agreed and while he couldn't wait to start on his project, he figured it might take him a couple weeks to put it together based on his basic mechanical skills. He started the project that night. He didn't realize how much stuff was missing until Fred gave him the list. The biggest things that were missing were the handlebars and brakes.

Within a week's time, he had assembled it. This was something that Denny was extremely proud of, but the true test would be when he fired it up. Denny had ridden on a couple motorcycles before, and of course his Whizzer, but this was the real deal; this was his motorcycle. There were quite a few older guys that hung around in the wash area behind the gas station. They had made couple helpful suggestions regarding his motorcycle. Quite a bit of 'American boy engineering' held his motorcycle together, which meant baling wire, luck, and Denny's brute force, but overall, Denny thought it was a solid effort.

Finally, he was ready to start up the motorcycle, but he didn't want to make a huge deal about it, in case it didn't start at all. Denny gassed it up, filled up the oil and was standing at the ready to kick start it. A certain sequence had to be followed to start it, which involved tinkering with the throttle, spark plugs, kicking it over a couple times, and on the second try he was able to start it without flooding it. He was so excited he ran to find Fred, who was just about as excited as Denny. The air was intoxicating, it was a mix of gas, oil, and grease or as he would forever remember the scent of a freshly finished job.

Denny had an ear-to-ear grin on his face. He accomplished something! There weren't many moments like this for him and he took time to bask in this triumph. As he sat on his bike, he thought about what this meant. Off the top of his head, it meant he would be more mobile. The top speed for his Whizzer was 30mph. This in turn, equated to more freedom. No longer would he be limited to the radius of San Bernardino; his horizons were expanding. His older friends told him once he got his motorcycle running, he should ride with them. At the top of the list was staying off the radar of cops because he still didn't have his license.

Denny's plan for showing off his new motorcycle included cruising the neighborhood and taking his buddies for rides on the back rack of the bike. Denny made sure the rack was secure because that's where girls would be riding—impressing girls was one of the main reasons he needed this motorcycle.

First though, Fred asked to ride it to check it out mechanically. When Fred got back, he was shaking his head and told him, "You need to be cautious because the brakes are very touchy and practically non-existent, but if you are careful not to speed around, it should be okay. You also need to take care on Kendall Drive where it goes over the mountain and also on Devils Canyon Road." When Fred was telling him this, he was motioning to the foothills directly behind the station and to the larger hills to the west. This all sounded like wise advice, however to a teenager who was now fully mobilized, it barely registered.

Denny already had his jacket, Levi's, and boots on and now with the Indian motorcycle, he was really styling. He had grown out his hair and wore it in a hairstyle called a D.A. or a duck's ass. It was a haircut where the top was super high, but the back was parted in the middle and then folded back to look like the butt of a duck, complete with wings that were combed back toward the middle part that went from the crown of his head to the nape of his neck. Everyone was wearing their hair this way, even the girls.

Denny had become acquainted rather well with his steady girl Duchess. They would hang out in the wash area, at McDonald's where they met, or ride around town in general. The next day he would cruise by and ask her to go out with him for a night on the town. This would consist of cruising E Street, parking at burger joints, cruising around some more and then heading up to the arroyos to party with his friends after curfew. Because the wash was in the county area, the city cops didn't bug them. No houses were close to the party spot, which meant no nosy neighbors were around to complain. It was like having your own private beach somewhere, with no ocean.

Denny and his friends had added a few items to their hideaway, including camping tables and beach chairs. Billy found a couple discarded nightstands that they hauled out to 'the spot.' As always, they kept their party stuff hidden away during the day. It wasn't uncommon after a night of revelry for the crew to fall asleep outside. Denny didn't need to worry about getting into trouble and the other boys' parents trusted them enough sometimes to camp out. They were only allowed to do this on the weekend and not on a school night. Besides, it was only a few blocks in any direction to each other's houses.

The crew was allowed the run of the neighborhood without too many rules.

Denny took a bit of time and finished cleaning up the mess from putting his motorcycle together. Since it was almost noon, he decided to run around showing off his Indian motorcycle. His first stop was at Terry's place, where he happened to be home. Terry wasn't as lucky as Denny and didn't have any height on him, so he couldn't manage the bike enough to take it for a test drive, but they went out for a little bit and went over to show off his new bike to Jim, Billy, and his new friend Johnny Thompson.

Eventually it was time to go back to work, so he dropped Terry off and headed back to the station. Fred waved hi to him and over the load noise of the Indian engine said, "How are you liking it?"

Again, Denny's grin was huge, and he said, "I'm liking it just fine! Thanks for all your help getting her running." Fred took off shortly and Denny worked the rest of the night till closing.

Denny was two weeks shy of his 16th birthday. After he closed up the station, he wanted to enjoy his accomplishment and take advantage of the weather. He planned to cruise out Route 66 to the west of town.

Riding out of town with the desert breeze blowing on his face and the moon lighting his path, he was happy. Young Denny had never been so content.

Chapter 28

Hanging Out and Staying Dry

For the fall of 1954, Denny planned to buckle down and concentrate on his grades. The other things that Denny was concentrating on were girls, having a good time, and drinking.

His circle of friends was increasing and in addition to his old crew he also started to spend more time with his friend Kenny, who lived over by San Bernardino High School. He owned a motorcycle too and would come over to 'the spot' on the weekends. Denny still bunked at his friends' houses in the north end, mainly with Jim Christie, but sometimes he switched off and on between Jim's place and Johnny Thompson's house depending on what was going on at night.

During the fall, every Friday and Saturday night, he was either cruising around town or gathering up friends, mostly girls, to party at 'the spot' after curfew. They wanted to keep it fairly small, no more than 20 people, so they didn't cause trouble or make a lot of noise. Everyone was aware of the loose rules and, remarkably, they hadn't been hassled by the cops at all.

Denny's friends were a mix of boys his age trying to be cool and some men who were cool. Nearly all of the guys Denny hung with rode some type of motorbike, either a real motorcycle or Whizzers. Jim had Denny's old Whizzer. The men who hung out were around ten years older than him and all owned motorcycles. Some of them had been in the military during World War II. Denny was too young to remember much of the war. The only exposure was his Aunt Ruthie who had been in the WAVES and his Uncle Chuck who served in the navy. Denny didn't have any stories to share. Most of the time, he sat and listened when they talked about what they went through and how they still had nightmares about being in the war.

Denny and the boys usually hung out with them only on weekend nights because the older guys had jobs they worked during the week. They talked about putting together a motorcycle club. There were a couple of guys who made and wore patches on their jackets with a skull and a wheel, but Denny wasn't into that sort of stuff, he didn't like any strings attached and he wasn't a joiner. He just wanted to relax and have a good time.

Denny enjoyed the older guys' company, but most of all enjoyed the beer they shared with him. Sometimes they would have these parties called 'beer busts.' These parties usually involved having a fire, drinking, smooching, and raising hell.

Denny and his school buddies were in charge of bringing the ladies out to the 'beer bust.' This wasn't hard to do because everyone was always looking for a party. Denny had his pickup lines down cold, so it was easy to persuade girls to go with him. The more adventurous girls would hop on the motorcycle, tuck in tight against the small of his back and were happy to get some wind in their hair. For Denny 'getting wind' was one of his favorite feelings.

The only thing that sidelined their fun was the rain.

On November 9, Denny figured out why the curbs on Sierra Way were so high. It rained for two days straight and when it finally stopped, it took about a week for things to dry out. It had rained so much that kids were taking their parents' row boats and floating down the streets. The water flowing down the north and south streets was higher than the curbs. In the Arrowhead Farms area, where Denny lived, the water ran as high as the top porch steps, about three feet high. Arrowhead Farms was a county area which meant there were no curbs to hold back water or funnel it down through town.

Denny was happy about sleeping in the garage as it was far enough back on the Christie's property to stay out of the water. This kind of rain was crazy and going to school sucked. One day, Jim's mom gave them a ride and one day he had to ride his motorcycle to school. As he rode, water came off the back tire and went up the back of his jacket and by the time he got to class he was drenched.

Rain was one thing, but when it rained here, it was awful. Denny didn't know why. Because he was nosy and curious, he wanted to find out more about all the water and why a day or two of rain wreaked so much havoc.

A couple of the men he hung out with on the weekends worked in construction. He asked them about the project along Sierra Way and 30th Street. He thought it might have something to do with water storage or sewers. There was a construction crew that had been digging up the road and building a system of tunnels. His friends couldn't tell him anything about it, but one of them said to go ask one of the workers on the job. He made it a point to tell Denny to wait till they were on break or at lunch though as job sites were strict about this.

Denny waited a week or so for them to dig out all the mud that had partially filled the newly built area of the tunnel and then after school for a few afternoons, he sat around watching them. He struck up a conversation with a couple of workers and one of them, Bill, seemed to know a lot about what was going on.

Over the course of a few days, on Bill's breaks, he laid out the scope of the project that was to take water from the foothill areas and direct it toward the Santa Ana riverbed in the downtown San Bernardino area over by the Sante Fe Depot area.

Bill said, "Most people don't know the Santa Ana River starts below Big Bear, 'up the hill,' and has a few offshoots that add to the river from the Mt. San Gorgonio area. All of this water makes the river larger until it reaches San Bernardino. One of the main contributors to the flooding problem in this region are the wildfires. San Bernardino is more or less a desert town; once the water comes off the mountains, it flows downhill. If the hills have been burned, there is no underbrush with root systems to hold and use the water and no place for the water to go. The hills become saturated and when this happens, you get mudslides and floods.

"At this rate with all the rain, then drought, then rain again, we will be building tunnels and places to catch water for a long time. Hell, I'll be retired, dead and gone, before they stop building systems for floods.

"We still need to contend with Lytle Creek. She's a monster too. Lytle Creek and the Santa Ana River provided a lot of water to San Bernardino. Almost all of the water in San Bernardino is under the city in artesian wells. This is where water percolates into the ground and stays. Los Angeles hasn't been able to tap into this water for their ever-growing needs and I hope the city keeps it that way.

"If you want to learn a trade people will always need, learn how to build stuff. What we are doing here is building infrastructure that will last 50 to 100 years. One day these tunnels will go all over the city, from the North End of San Bernardino all the way to Colton. This is my mark on the world, my contribution. If you learn a trade, you will feel like you are part of something greater than yourself."

Denny left Bill that afternoon with quite a bit to think about. Sure, Denny had his own troubles, but Bill was helping solve problems and building for a future that he may never see completed. This took Denny outside of himself and got him thinking about society and not just the fact that it sucked to be riding his motorcycle in the rain.

The next day Denny stopped by one last time as he was beginning to understand the city's relationship with water. Bill was working and came over and chatted with Denny when he had a free minute.

Bill said he forgot to mention a couple things. "People around these parts have a love-hate relationship with water. Ask anyone who lives on Sierra Way. That street is the main watershed street for the rain that flows off the foothills. The Mormons built it that way. That's why the curbs are so high. Since 1927, they've made footbridges in all different shapes and sizes so the kids on the east side of town would be able to go to their schools on the west side of Sierra Way. If you don't believe me, ask the old timers, or hell, anyone who went to elementary school in the 40s. These footbridges would go from the middle of the street to the sidewalk to let the kids cross. Some versions of these bridges would swing out to the street and then swing back to the curb to let cars pass. It's a real production when it rains. What we are doing here will hopefully stop that from happening."

Denny said, "Hey Bill, thanks for telling me all that stuff. I appreciate it. I don't know what I am going to be or do in my life, but you got me thinking about things bigger than me. It helps me out. I didn't tell you my story, but I'm on my own and I wanted to thank you for taking the time to tell me what you are doing here and how it will make a difference in the future." Denny threw out his hand and Bill shook it. As he left, he waved and headed out a little wiser about water and infrastructure.

Chapter 29

Messing Around and Christmas

During this time, Denny wasn't working as much at the gas station, only one or two days a week, but he was doing a little side business. He would visit all the mechanic shops and other gas stations in the North End and on Route 66 to see if they needed any help plugging tires and fixing flats. This gave him more free time. Some of the older guys taught him how to steal hub caps and car stereos for spare cash and where to sell them. He wasn't proud of any of this, but it was easier money than working his ass off and it gave him more free time.

Denny never got caught stealing anything; he wasn't stupid about it and if he couldn't pull the job in less than two minutes, he didn't do it. Denny made a point to never break any windows or damage the interiors of cars to steal the stereos. People always left their cars unlocked so it was easy pickings. Briefcases, files, and anything else kept in the cars were off-limits for him. Not so much a code, but it made him feel better about taking the stereos that he didn't deserve.

Fred gave Denny some flack about his new schedule. "I don't want you to go off the rails here. You are doing pretty well, and your grades have improved, but the constant partying and whatever else you're doing will catch up with you. I'm not preaching to you; I am trying to save you from making mistakes."

Denny took it to heart, "Don't worry about me, Fred. I'm having a good time right now; it will be okay. For most of my life, I've been pushed around and had to go and do whatever the adults wanted me to do. Right now, I am enjoying not having them around."

Denny reluctantly agreed to go to Chuck and Fran's house for Christmas Eve and to Milt's for Christmas Day. He went over on his own and made sure he cleaned up for the day. When he arrived, he was the first guest. It was pleasing to have a little one-on-one time with Chuck before he got too busy hosting everyone. Chuck asked him, "How are you doing on your own? It can't be easy."

"I'm doing okay. Have you seen my new ride?"

"I haven't seen it, but I did hear it. What kind of motorcycle is that?"

"It's kind of a 'mish mash' of an Indian, 1947, rigid frame and other parts to make it run. I parked it on the street in case it leaks oil."

It was a pedestrian conversation, but a bonding one. Chuck and Denny went outside and took a look at the motorcycle and Chuck commented, "I've never had a desire to ride a motorcycle but sounds like you love it." To which Denny nodded his head.

Shortly after showing his Indian motorcycle to Chuck, Denny heard his mom come into the house. He had been in the bathroom, but he could hear her boisterous call out to everyone. Margo came up to Denny gushingly and for show said, "How about a kiss and hug for your old ma?" Denny obliged her with a hug and kiss on the cheek, and then distanced himself from her by sitting at the end of the couch on the corner in case he needed to extricate himself. Being trapped on a sectional couch by a coffee table and a bunch of people, particularly Margo, wasn't Denny's idea of fun.

Around her siblings and their families, his mom maintained a pleasant demeanor. She usually hung around outside smoking wherever she was, so it was easy to avoid her. Eugene wasn't around, which was just fine. Denny didn't ask, but he wondered where he was. The adults toasted to the holiday season and each person including Denny opened one gift, as this was a family tradition for Christmas Eve. This year, he got cash, which was always handy and greatly appreciated.

Denny wasn't surprised the next day to hear that Eugene was in the hospital. Apparently he had gotten in a major accident on Christmas Eve on his way over to Chuck's. His mother was not at Milt's to ask about what happened, but his Uncles Milt and Chuck filled Denny in on the situation. They told him the accident was in the paper.

Eugene was under arrest at Community Hospital. He had been drunk and drove from his lane into oncoming traffic. A mother and daughter were in the hospital because of him. The details were awful, as both of the ladies hit the windshield. Everyone was expected to live, but Eugene wasn't going anywhere for a while. Another car had been involved, with a dad driving and his three kids. Thank God nothing happened to them.

Denny felt sorry for the families involved. Who needed this shit on Christmas Eve? Still, he didn't give one fuck about Eugene. What a dumb ass that guy was.

Margo called a little later that day and asked to speak with Denny. She was crying hysterically on the phone. Through her tears, she exclaimed, "I don't know what to do. They won't let me talk to him and he has a broken leg, and his arm is in a cast."

Denny was cold to her and said, "He's a piece of shit and you should leave him, I hope he rots in jail."

Margo said, "Go to hell Denny!"

Denny retorted, "Eugene first, Mom, Eugene first." Of course, she immediately slammed down the phone. This was her expected, typical response to everything when she was backed up against a wall and didn't get her way.

His family was always welcoming to him, and when he was with them, he knew he was loved, but just like before, he had to go back to reality after the holiday parties.

After his school Christmas vacation, the parties in the wash stopped for a while, because it was too damn cold for the Californians.

Chapter 30

Down The Steps Again

Denny's grades were up, and he was making it on his own. Eugene had been sentenced to state prison for his drunk driving accidents and Margo had moved on to other men, even though she was still married to Eugene. Things were great in February of 1955, so it really surprised Denny he chose to ride his 1947 Indian down the halls of San Bernardino High School's Admin Building that day.

Denny was trying to find Epsy, his girlfriend, and he planned to pick her up after class. As Denny rode through the entry way, he was shocked by how loud his motorcycle was. The exhaust from his bike echoed throughout the building, and anyone who had been in the hall scrambled out of the way by the time he had entered. As he was rolling through, he figured out this was a bad idea and headed for the exit. Denny forgot about the flight of stairs directly outside the doors and miscalculated his ability to navigate them. He could feel that he was losing control and he ended up dumping his bike on the steps.

Based on his previous experience with steps, he should've known better than to try and ride these stairs down. Denny was attempting to pick up the Indian when he noticed he was being watched. As he looked up, several teachers and students were staring down at him. He knew he was in trouble when the vice principal, Mr. Ingli, showed up looking pissed. Mr. Ingli always wore a grimace, but his face was especially dour that day. Denny peered up at him and sheepishly stammered out an apology. Epsy was in the crowd, smiling at him, along with some of the other girls. The ladies really did love the bad boys.

Mr. Ingli demanded, "Save the apology for later. Right now I need you to park your bike and follow me to the office."

Denny did as instructed. The walk over was very quiet. Mr. Ingli was not to be trifled with; he was known as a strict disciplinarian.

Denny sat outside in the chairs waiting for the principal and vice principal to confer about the situation and by the sound of it, he was in the shit. His mom had also joined the meeting.

When he was at last summoned into the principal's office, Margo was there in all her glory. She was sitting in her classic 'Margoesque' pose with that fucking smile-smirk on her face and her arms folded like he had disappointed her. Truth be told, she had been disappointing him his whole life, so turnabout was fair play.

The principal, Mr. Webster, who Denny had never talked to before, gave him a preachy lecture peppered with "this is very serious," "you could have killed someone" and "this is very irresponsible" to which Denny only paid attention to the snippets when Mr. Webster got excited in his speech and raised his voice. The part he did listen to was at the end when he said, "Denny Halvorsen, we are going to suspend you from school and more than likely expel you, but before we do, we are going to send you to the school psychologist. According to your mother here, you are incorrigible. We need to figure out how we can help you change your behavior. An assessment will help us figure out what our next steps for you will be." With that he called in the counselor to make the appointment and Denny was to report back to school in two days minus the motorcycle.

His mom was suspiciously quiet during the oratory and scowled through the whole thing, trying to look matronly.

For show, she started talking to Denny, as they were leaving the office, but as soon as they were out of earshot, she stopped, threw up her hands, and said, "You're on your own."

Denny bristled and told her straight up, "I've been on my own for a very long time." With that Denny walked over to his bike and headed over to the gas station to talk with Fred for a while.

When Denny settled in for the night, he had a long think about where he was headed. After talking to Fred, he was beginning to realize just how fucked he was. Fred had empathized, "I've been suspended before, who hasn't? Being expelled is something else entirely. I am not sure what school you will go to now. They will either send you to Pacific or Colton High School."

He didn't understand why he pulled that stunt. Maybe it was his way of asking for help or getting someone to pay attention to him. Sure, his friends thought he was the coolest guy ever for what he did, but Denny knew different. Everything in his whole life up to this point indicated he was a loser. From the time his third-grade teacher wrote on his report card, "This student will never amount to anything" and all of the crap with his mom, his dad, Bob Ertell and all the other fucking people in his life, so far everything showed his teacher had been right. That night and the next night, he cried himself to sleep in the dark with racking sobs.

Chapter 31

IQ Test

Denny was back at school and talking to the district school psychologist, who operated out of the county. Mr. Ashurst introduced himself and asked Denny, "Have you ever had an IQ test?"

Denny said, "No, what's an IQ test?"

The shrink told him, "It's an intelligence test that can tell me, regardless of your education, how smart you are."

Denny thought this man was cool. Mr. Ashurst told Denny he wanted to do an interview first. He started quizzing Denny about his background, how he was raised, where he had lived, it was an incredibly detailed interview. Denny told him the truth, how his dad had an FBI file, and his mom wasn't much of a mother. How Bob had beat him. Denny gave him all of the details about his life, including the many schools he had attended and where they were located. When they were done talking about his background, Mr. Ashurst administered the test.

Denny took his time on the test. It was interesting; he had never been asked these types of questions before. The test was one on one and some of the questions were complicated. This part of the test took about an hour and a half. When they were done, he was told to go ahead and take a break while the test was being evaluated.

When Mr. Ashurst came back into the room, he had a huge smile on his face. He announced, "You have the highest IQ I have ever tested. It's off the scale. There is nothing in this world you couldn't do if you wanted to."

Denny sat for a moment and stared at him, and he began smiling too.

Then he advised, "If I were you, I would use your given name, not your stepdad's name. I would go by Doug Dulin. This will do wonders for your self-esteem, and since that was your given name, it will give you an identity, your own identity."

Denny, now Doug, kept shaking Mr. Ashurst's hand and saying thank you before he left.

When Doug stepped out of the school's admin building, he felt like a million bucks. This was the best news he had ever received. He didn't know what this meant for him at that moment, but his future appeared to be a little brighter and Douglas Dennis Dulin was walking just a little bit taller.

Chapter 32

Doug

The transition from Denny to Doug was going well. His friends all adapted to his name fairly easily and there weren't too many questions about him wanting to be called Doug now. He had told them since he was starting over at Colton High School, he wanted to change some things.

Doug was a different person when he started going to Colton High School. His sense of worth was definitely on the rise. His reputation had preceded him and quite a few people seemed to be aware of him riding his motorcycle in the halls at San Bernardino High School. It afforded him an instant cool factor, but Doug tried to maintain a lower profile at Colton High.

He was also learning what a piece of shit his motorcycle was. On Sundays, Doug would take rides to different places. This particular Sunday he rode up to the high desert via Route 66 through Hesperia to Victorville. On the way back 'down the hill' on Blue Cut Road, Doug could feel his bike slipping out from under him. His tires must have hit an oil slick, which was bad because his bike's brakes were non-existent. He was traveling about 70mph when he started to slide sideways down the road. Doug wasn't sure what to do so he stayed with it and rode it out and was able to right the bike again.

Immediately after he recovered from the slide, he pulled over to catch his breath. This close call literally scared the shit out of him. Doug had to walk over and take a dump in the bushes, right by the side of the road. Things could have turned out worse, as he only wore a leather jacket, 501 jeans, and boots for protection from road rash. It took him a while to get back on his motorcycle and head out. That was the closest he had come to a bad accident.

Another time Doug was riding in the wash area where they partied, which was roughly the size of two or three city blocks. It was during the day, and he was dirt biking with his Indian. Doug started up a hill, which he thought continued down as a slope on the other side, but it was actually a cliff. The pegs on his bike had been worn down to sharp points on both sides of the frame from leaning into curves.

Doug drove over the hill and by the time he realized he wasn't going to have a soft landing, his bike landed on top of him. It wasn't until he tried to pull the bike off him, he realized one of the pegs was stuck in his left leg, halfway down his calf. He hated to ask for help, but he yelled over to buddies, and a few of them came over. Jim stared at him, scratched his head, and pointed out that Doug was bleeding quite a bit. Doug motioned to the motorcycle and managed to stammer out, "Yep, can you help me pull this fucker off me?" They all worked together and were able to pull the bike off.

Doug took off his pants and examined his leg. An inch to either side he would have cracked his bone, but he must have missed it.

Jim asked, "Are you going to go to the doctor?

"Let's head back to the house so I can clean this up and look at it. I don't have money for a doctor." Amazingly, his bike was okay as his leg took the brunt of the hit. He gingerly hopped back on, still in his underwear, and they rode the short distance to Jim's place.

Jim got to the house first and ran inside to talk to his mom. She told Doug to come in, take a bath, and to pay particular attention to cleaning the area around the wound. He followed her advice and borrowed some of Jim's shorts and a clean shirt and came out of the bathroom when he was done.

Jim's mom, Mrs. Christie, was strangely calm, which helped Doug's anxiety level. She took charge and had him sit on the edge of the tub with his leg resting on the toilet while she poured alcohol into the hole and meticulously cleaned his wound. Once she was done, she put a large bandage on it. She assured him, "This may hurt a lot right now, but if you keep it clean and bandaged you should be okay. The wound is deep, but the surface skin is not too damaged." With that advice, she handed him the box of bandages, a bottle of rubbing alcohol and told him to keep it and make sure his leg stayed clean and dry.

Doug's leg healed up in a month and in no time, he was back up to snuff.

The last sucky thing that happened to him that made his butt clench was when he took a ride through the vineyards. Doug followed Kendall Drive out and took an old tractor road to the right, heading north. Along this road there was nothing but grape vineyards that stretched all the way to the foothills. A recent addition to his motorcycle were 'ape hanger' handlebars. He was tall and he liked using them when he was riding. On that day he was cruising on a slow ride, basking in the sun when he attempted to avoid a rut in the road. Doug pulled up on the bars to avoid it and just after he cleared it the handlebars popped off in his hands, he lost control and he wound up dumping his bike.

Since he was out in the middle of nowhere, he just laid there, in the road, for a couple minutes collecting himself and taking inventory of his body. Nothing was broken and he was okay except for some scrapes. Doug had to figure out how to get his bike back to the station and put some handlebars on it, but he would stay away from the 'ape hangers' going forward.

When he finally got his bike back to the station via a pickup truck, he asked Fred, "What do you think made these come off?"

Fred imparted his wisdom, "Gravity and a cold weld, that's what happened." It was funny thinking about it later, but not so much that day.

The rest of the school year was uneventful. Doug wasn't sure if knowing he was smart was why his grades improved, or if he was applying himself to school more that made the difference, but at the end of the school year in June, Doug had a report card of solid B's. Not only was he surprised, but he felt proud of this accomplishment. Even his new school counselor gave him an atta-boy for his efforts. His mom would have received his report card at work, but she didn't mention anything to him about it, until his birthday. She had moved over to a house south of Marshall and west of E Street. She asked him to come over for dinner as a means to make amends for not speaking to him these past months.

Doug didn't dress for the occasion; he was beyond trying to impress her. As he came up to the house, he noticed a new man with his mom. She introduced him, but he didn't bother to remember his name. He was yet another annoyance for Doug to deal with. Margo kept calling him Denny and he kept correcting her to Doug.

She finally asked, "Why the change?"

"That's my name, that's why I am using Doug or Douglas. You are the one who named me, and I don't think I should need to justify that to you, but I want to be called by my real first and last name."

"Alright, Mr. Douglas Dennis Dulin, we are grilling steaks tonight especially for your birthday. Sit here for a little bit and we will be eating shortly."

The rest of the evening passed without incident and his present from his mom was exactly nothing, just a steak dinner, but at least it was a delicious steak and was better than no acknowledgement at all.

Chapter 33

Champagne Anyone?

Doug was back to his partying ways with his crew in the north end 'beer busting' on the weekends at 'the spot.' It was really hard to believe no one had rousted them from it. It was a known place for kids to come and party, but by invitation only. Sure, they had to run some of the younger kids off, but it never turned into anything mean, it was more or less just telling them they were too young to hang out with them.

The only problem with these parties was sometimes they would run out of alcohol and, if the guys of age weren't around to make a beer run, they had to be creative, which was the situation in October of 1955. Doug and Johnny were self-appointed to secure more alcohol.

Doug thought he could score some booze. They rode down 40th Street to the Arrowhead Country Club off Valencia Avenue. They kept alcohol in a little building over by the pool to supply the main club house bar and restaurant. To be stealthy they parked their bikes away from the main building and snuck up the greens toward the shed. They had brought a hammer with them. Johnny knocked the lock off the door and once inside they grabbed a case of champagne.

They took off running and as they were escaping the night watchman came out yelling after them. He said, "I have a gun and I'm not afraid to use it!"

To Doug and Johnny's disbelief, he fired a round off over their heads. They both stopped, dropped, and rolled into the closest sand trap. The man came over to where they were and said, "Get your asses out of that trap; we're going to the office to call the cops."

For the second time this year, Doug had fucked up bad. For all the times he had taken something that wasn't his or misappropriated alcohol, he had never been caught. Johnny and Doug sat quietly while the groundskeeper made the call to the cops. They had only been sitting for about five minutes when two cruisers rolled up, cuffed them, and took each of them away in separate cars.

Doug thought, 'Well this is it; my life is basically over. I'll end up in jail or even worse, prison.' But this time it wasn't for hitchhiking, they had been caught red-handed. The patrolman played up how he was going to go to jail and possibly prison for this, and it was a shame because he was such a young kid.

At the station, he had to speak with the desk sergeant. This cop was a notorious crusty asshole, who used to patrol the city on a trike, and he didn't take any shit.

He said, "The way I see it, you're going before the judge on Monday, or you're going in the army."

Doug told the sarge, "Well I've never been the army before, what do I need to do to sign up?"

"Do you have a birth certificate?"

"I don't have one."

"Well, your parents can sign an affidavit stating your age and that would be good enough."

Doug and the patrol officer went back outside, and he sat in the back of the squad car. He asked the cop, "What the hell is an after David?"

The cop laughed and said, "What the fuck are you talking about? After David? Oh, he meant affidavit, that's where your parents write down you are over 18 and they sign it."

"Why hell, I can do that." He wrote on a pad of paper exactly what he was told to and at the bottom he signed his mom's name.

They walked back into the station and showed the sergeant the paperwork and he said, "That'll do."

With that, Doug became the guest of the city for three nights.

Chapter 34

Packing Up and Shipping Out

On Tuesday morning, the cops took Doug to the recruiting station, where he showed the recruiter the affidavit with his 'mom's signature.' He said, "That's exactly what I need." Doug was handed a stack of forms to fill out. Once he was done with that stack of paperwork, he spent the next couple hours taking tests and by 4pm that day, he had signed up for a three-year stint in the army.

The recruiter told him he was required to report to the recruiting office on Friday but was given a couple days to say his goodbyes to everyone. Jim Christie came by and picked him up and told him that his motorcycle was at his house. "After you and Johnny left the party and didn't come back, we tried to retrace your steps and found your motorcycles the next day. Your bike is at my house." When they arrived at Jim's place, they sat on the front porch talking.

Instead of telling Jim the whole story about the arrest, he blurted out, "Jim! I'm going in the army on Friday."

Jim sat speechless for a full minute and then said, "Why?"

"If I hadn't joined, I would still be in jail. I seriously fucked up and if I didn't join, I would be going to prison. I wanted to tell you how much it means to me to have a friend like you. I haven't had many friends growing up and spending this time with you guys, my crew has been some of the best times in my life."

Jim gave Doug a hug and both of them knew what they dare not say, 'Things would never be the same again.'

Doug made his rounds, spoke with his other friends, and had similar conversations with them about their friendships, all of which were heartfelt and somber. Johnny's parents had put him on lockdown since he got out of jail and Doug was unable to see him before he left for the army.

When he went to see Fred, it was a difficult conversation. He hadn't visited Fred much lately, but he wanted to let him know what was going on. Fred came over, "Hey kid, how are you doing?"

Doug explained what had happened and Fred's face showed disappointment and then hope.

"You are a smart guy and I think joining the army will be one of the best things you ever do. You've had awful hard time this past few years and this might be what pushes you over the hill to being your own man. Once you are in the army, keep your head down, be thankful for three square meals and you'll be fine."

Doug took this advice to heart, he gave Fred a long hug, as he pulled away, he said, "Thank you for everything you have done for me, and I am sorry if sometimes I didn't listen, but you have truly helped me more than you will ever know." Doug waved again and got on his bike and headed out waving a last goodbye to Fred.

Although he was excited about his new path in life, he was melancholy about leaving San Bernardino and all of his buddies behind. This had been the one place he had allowed himself to put down some roots and have a sense of belonging. Doug stayed at Jim's until he left on Friday, but he had some late nights not partying, but staying awake and thinking about what the future would bring. One thing that gave him solace was his mother would not be in the army and he wouldn't be bothered with her petty bullshit for at least three years.

Doug sold his motorcycle, packed everything in the same suitcase he had used for his trip to California, and by Friday he was on the bus headed to Los Angeles.

PART IV
LIFE ABROAD

You're in the army now,
You're not behind a plow.
You'll never get rich,
You son of a bitch,
You're in the army now.
(Taylor & Olsen "We're In The army Now,"
chorus verse 1).
(Words modified by countless recruits)

Chapter 35

Arrival at Fort Ord

From the recruiting station, Doug took a bus to Los Angeles. Once he got off the bus, all the recruits were guided to a multi-story office building where they would take the Armed Services Enlistment Oath. As Doug was saying the oath, he was starting to realize the gravity of what he was doing. "I, Douglas Dennis Dulin, do solemnly swear that I will support and defend the Constitution of the United States against all enemies, foreign or domestic; that I will bear true faith and allegiance to the same; that I take this obligation freely, without any mental reservation or purpose of evasion; and that I will well and faithfully discharge the duties of the office on which I am about to enter. So help me God."

Doug had what can only be described as an 'out of body' experience after taking the oath, which lasted for about ten minutes. The recruits were told they would stay in a hotel next to the train station and needed to report at 7am, the next morning, for a train that was leaving at 8am. The train would take them to Salinas, where buses would then take them to Fort Ord.

Doug took full advantage of having a cozy bed to sleep in. Each recruit had a roommate, but Doug didn't chat too much with his. There was sure to be some kind of bullshit coming his way the next several weeks and Doug didn't want to get distracted, so he made sure he caught up on his sleep so he would be well rested.

At Union Station the next morning, while waiting for the train to take him to Salinas Doug listened to a group of recruits chatter. These guys were a year or two older than him, but far less worldly as in they had probably never had sex, lived on their own, or had stolen anything in their young lives. They were mainly scared, but Doug was more optimistic about the future. From what he heard, it was going to be tough for about eight weeks and after basic training was over, he would go to classes to learn his military occupational specialty, or MOS.

Doug wasn't worried too much about boot camp as he had been to two military schools at a younger age, and he was able to assimilate well into that environment. The Korean War was recently over and if the United States could stay out of another war, his three years should fly by.

His plans included getting his GED, the equivalent to a high school diploma. Passing the 'Tests of General Education Development' were considered the same as graduating from high school. Doug also wanted to take some college courses so when he got out, he could take full advantage of the GI Bill. The army was a chance for Doug to better himself.

His grandpa's advice a few years before was coming back to him and he hoped he could make him proud. Doug wondered where he would be stationed. He wanted to broaden his horizons, leave the boy behind, and become a man of the world.

Doug was jostled out of his daydreaming by one of the guys announcing, "Hey, it's time to catch the train!"

Doug wanted to try and get some sleep on the train, which is why he picked a window seat where he could rest his head. They were going to be on the train for seven or eight hours, and he was going to get some shut-eye.

The motion of the train lulled Doug into a deep sleep. He woke up as they passed Summerland and stayed awake to take in the spectacle of California. The farthest north Doug had been on the California coast was Santa Barbara with Bob Ertell on his 'apology tour.'

These beaches were something millions of people wanted to visit but not everyone was lucky enough to see them firsthand. 'How fortunate am I to be here at this moment, living life?' He took in the coastal scenery for about an hour and then fell back asleep until they stopped in Salinas. Doug was thankful he had been able to nap and hoped the extra sleep would help him face whatever he was in for when he got off the train. As they pulled into the Salinas station, he took a couple of deep breaths and prepped himself for what was next.

The first thing Doug picked up on as he exited the train was that this was a podunk place with an extremely small train station. The second thing was a group of army guys who had gathered and were about to do something which he thought might involve him. The recruits he was traveling with congregated, and Doug did not want to be singled out, so he kind of moved into the middle of the group as this was no time to stand out in the crowd. Two things he had learned in military school were to pay attention and try not to bring unnecessary scrutiny to yourself. Fairly quickly they were directed to board a bus and to give the person at the door their name, which is what he did, he also included 'sir' with every conversation for good measure.

Doug found a window seat on the army bus headed to Fort Ord and sat back and looked around. There was a mix of guys from diverse backgrounds. Because no one was in a uniform yet, this bus could have been a team going somewhere to play a high school sports game or a bunch of people going on a field trip. Doug wasn't going to make a lot of friends on the bus. It was best not to make the effort, as soon as they got to the base, he anticipated they would be moved again before they got settled.

They were only on the bus for about 15 minutes when it came to a stop at the main gate of Fort Ord. They took a circuitous route to a cluster of buildings that were probably barracks. When the bus stopped, they were yelled off the bus, which Doug expected, and they were told to pick up the pace. They were walking/running to a building with a lot of bunks in it, which Doug assumed was where they would be staying.

Once they all assembled, a sergeant instructed them how to make a bed, which seemed to be critically important, so he paid close attention to make sure he could master it. They were issued bed linens and told to make their bunks up. After they were done with this task, they were told what to expect the next day, which would include receiving haircuts, uniforms, duffle bags along with more forms and tests, but that first night, they would eat and go to sleep. The next day he would start going through the paces of switching over from civilian life to a soldier's life.

As Doug lay in his bunk, he thought, 'I can do this and for at least three years, I don't have to worry about food or a bed to sleep in.' These thoughts alone took a huge weight off his shoulders and Doug slept the sleep of a tired puppy.

Chapter 36

Boot Camp

Doug was used to getting up early, so it didn't bother him when they got up at 6am. They were instructed to shit, shower, and shave and to be ready to go by 7am. They were still in their civilian clothes as they boarded the bus to go to eat breakfast, after which they promptly received a haircut. Before that though, they were given $20, which was exciting, but the sergeants called it a 'flying 20' and Doug figured out that the $20 was going to disappear quickly, as they paid a buck and a quarter for a haircut, a dollar for the clothes marking kit and more money for other various personal things they needed. They didn't have to pay for all the standard issue stuff like uniforms, but by the end of the two days, he had a feeling there would be very little left.

Perhaps it was because Doug had been to military school before—or could have been because he was ready for someone to take care of him—he had no problems in boot camp. While he wasn't the best recruit, he kept his head down and did as he was told. There was a lot to learn. Most of it was interesting stuff about map reading, shooting, and cleaning his issued M-1 rifle. Some of the things he didn't learn were how to march, protect himself from venereal disease, and how to peel potatoes. All of these skills he had mastered elsewhere.

Quite a few of the recruits were having issues with basic things like discipline, shining shoes, and keeping their stuff squared away. Others would cry in their bunks at night because they were homesick. This was an unfamiliar feeling to Doug, as other than missing his friends, he didn't have much to be sad about. This was going to be an adventure and he was going to make the most of it.

It was almost November and, because they were so close to the coast, it was cold every day. Doug had become acclimated to California weather, so at this point, even though the temperature was only in the forties, it was now cold to him. One bonus that almost made up for the cold was being able to see the ocean every day.

The things other recruits were complaining about were petty, like the food. The meals in Doug's opinion were great compared to living on sandwiches or hot dogs. So far, he hadn't had a bad meal yet.

Doug looked forward to his meals. Breakfast was amazing, consisting of cereal, Wheaties, Grape Nuts or some type of porridge, and eggs. Lunch, or as the military called it dinner and dinner was called supper for some reason, both of which were substantial meals with interchangeable menus. The list of food seemed to be endless, roast shoulder, pork chops, spareribs, meat loaf, etc. There were no bad meals in basic. Doug never complained and was super excited when they got deviled eggs or soft dinner rolls. This may sound like basic sustenance to some, but to him, it was amazing that there were three meals and plenty of food.

Recruits worked hard in basic. The first three weeks were very tough physically. Doug got into the rhythm of all the sit ups, chin ups and daily exercise routines and drills and was feeling strong. He scored well on the rifle range and could take his weapon apart blindfolded if needed. Doug was constantly cleaning his gun and shining his brass and shoes when he was in the barracks. Unlike the other recruits, he hadn't been dressed down yet by his drill sergeant and didn't plan on making himself a target.

Doug was changing. He was more confident in his abilities and started to feel like he might be able to make something of himself. Sure, he was still on constant alert because he didn't want to do any stupid shit, like some of the recruits, but it wasn't hard, it was actually easy for him. His platoon was able to go into town at the end of their fourth week of basic training, which was a treat. A bus took them to Salinas for a Saturday night out, but they were required to be back by 11pm.

Saturday night a couple of guys invited him to go with them to the tattoo shop. Since he wasn't of drinking age, he wasn't able to cut loose like he did with his buddies in San Bernardino, so he planned to go with them. Doug wasn't going to get a tattoo, but he would accompany the other recruits while they waited for tattoos, and wouldn't you know it, they both chickened out. It was funny because they were excited to do it, but when it came down to the ink meeting the arm, they were super worried about what their parents would say. It also didn't help that the guys coming out of the parlor were whining about how much it hurt and complaining about how painful it would be to do push-ups.

After leaving the tattoo parlor, they went out walking around and checking out the town of Salinas. There wasn't much to see in town. Everyone was talking about James Dean, who had died on his way to the Salinas Sports Car Races which had been held at the airport the beginning of October. Doug hadn't heard a lot about James Dean, only that he was in a movie, *East of Eden*, but the kids in town were still talking about the accident that had happened at the end of September.

Doug was wondering why this small town was so busy and he learned that Salinas was a hub city that had a nomadic population due to the surrounding agricultural communities as well as transitory military personnel from Fort Ord. On any given weekend the town was hopping with both foot and car traffic. Some of the nearby students would go to the soldiers club on base to listen to bands that would play there.

The only incident during this time that pissed him right the fuck off was when he received his first paycheck. He only got about $25. Twenty was taken out for the 'flying twenty,' but it was still a lot less than he expected. His sergeant directed him to the company commander regarding his. After a few days, he was told that his mother had filed as a dependent and, as such, was entitled to half his pay. Doug couldn't believe this was legal; he thought he was well rid of her. He was going to do whatever it took to get her off his back. Not only was he 17, but now he had her sponging off him. This was the same person who left him alone most of his life and now this. It was unforgiveable.

Doug kept his cool and wits about him as he didn't want this situation with his mom to derail him. Just when he was feeling like he was free of her, she had found a way to dig her claws back into him. She was like a vampire, she sucked the life out of her victims, but he didn't want that to happen to him; he had to find a way to make this work. No one would ever understand her and why she was so conniving and heartless to her own son. The good news, if there was any, was that he was being taken care of in the army and didn't want for anything. Saving up money for his future was going to be a lot harder than he thought but he would make his way.

Doug would be graduating right before Christmas and chose not to invite her to the graduation or talk to her at all. His holidays would be spent on base. 'Fuck Margo.'

Doug wrote to his Aunt Babe, his uncles and grandpa. When he updated them on how he was doing there was no mention of his mom or what she had done. He told them he was okay and would be out of basic training shortly and he would keep them posted if he moved to another base. The next phase for him would be training for the Signal Corp and his MOS was 1649. This meant he was going to take a class called fixed station radio repair course, although he didn't know where those classes would take place. While he was at Fort Ord, he kept his head down and his eyes on the prize of completing basic.

Chapter 37

Signal School and NYC

Doug was keen on this next phase of training. He had just arrived at Fort Monmouth in New Jersey for his signal corp classes. Since he had finished basic training, he was given a few more privileges and he was able to live more of a normal type of life, if being in the military was normal.

Twenty-five percent of the population of military personnel were required to stay on base each weekend depending on where their last name fell in the alphabet. This meant Doug enjoyed leave three out of the four weekends a month. During Doug's class schedule there would be two holidays, Memorial Day, and Independence Day.

As with basic training, Doug chose to apply himself in class to guarantee he graduated from signal school without any issues. The classes were set up to have a proficiency test every week and it was fairly relaxed compared to basic training. All but a few of the instructors were civilians, so they were nowhere near as strict as the military instructors.

The one thing Doug didn't want to do was to climb the telephone pole. If you failed the proficiency test, one time you were put behind by a week. If you failed a second time, you would be behind your original class by two weeks, but the third time, you would wash out of the signal corps and be transferred to a Georgia base to learn how to climb telephone poles. Doug had decided there would be no pole climbing for him!

Doug would go off base occasionally, but only to local areas. Usually on the weekends he would go to the beach for a couple of hours after he was done studying. One of his favorite things to do was to go swimming at the pool on base. He would swim laps, usually for 40 minutes or a mile, and quiz himself about the various things he was trying to memorize for his classes while he was in the pool. Swimming at a steady rhythm allowed his mind to drift to another place where he did some of his best thinking. He solved a lot of problems in the water. Not only was he relaxed when he got out of the pool, but he was more at peace with himself and his situation. Swimming was a great stress reliever.

One weekend Doug and some of his new buddies, Paul, Benny, and James, planned to go to New York City. They all went in on a room for Saturday night and hit the town early Saturday morning. The base was only about an hour away from the city.

Since they were all underage, the only activities they could participate in was sightseeing, so they walked all over

Manhattan. They went to the Empire State Building, the Statue of Liberty, and Central Park. Sure, Doug had been to Chicago, but New York was a completely different experience. None of them realized how tall the Empire State Building was until they were outside on the observation deck or how enormous the Statue of Liberty was, or that you could go all the way up to the crown of the 'green lady.' Doug had never spent any time thinking about history in his young life but being in New York City made ponder the history of the country and how many people moved in and out of 'the city' on any given day.

The Empire State Building was the only scary part of the trip, and it was okay to be scared because it was the tallest building in the world, but at least he could say he'd been there. Doug was sure when he mentioned they had been to New York City, people would run through a checklist of tourist traps such as, "Did you go to the Empire State Building? How about the Statue of Liberty? Times Square? Central Park? The subway?" Check, check, check, check, and check.

Central Park was huge. They didn't walk through the park but skirted it instead. Doug stopped and played a pick-up game of chess. His uncles and grandpa taught him how to play. He was good at chess, or so he had been told. The older man he was playing with at the park, however, must have been a grand master or something because he kicked his ass in five moves. Doug imagined that's all the geezer did, sit in the park, play chess, and beat young, cocky kids that had the balls to challenge him, but Doug bowed to his abilities.

They took the subway to Times Square. They soaked it all in: the newsstands, people handing out cards for Broadway shows, people peddling their wares, counterfeit and legit, to make a buck. As the night started to fall, Doug spotted several pickpockets working the crowds, and one of them got pinched by a cop. The army did a good job explaining the need to keep your wallet in the front pocket of your pants due to thieves in large cities, especially New York.

Doug continued to read the crowd and watched from a doorway. From his perch he could see his buddies walking around and taking in all of the madness. They were all fading in energy after a while, so they headed back to their hotel before it got dark, and they too became targets. Closer to their hotel they popped into a deli and got food to take back to the room. Tucked safely in for the night, they played cards and generally acted stupid until about eleven, when one by one they knocked out.

Always an early riser, Doug got up the next morning, walked around a bit and got bagels and cream cheese for the guys. This type of city living was not for him; he didn't care if he ever returned to New York again. People in Manhattan were in a constant rush, rude as hell, and packed into buildings and trains like sardines. The sheer concentration of the population was deafening, suffocating, and maybe even deadly in some cases. At least in other places, like Southern California, people could spread out and not be in each other's business like they were in New York.

When he got back to the hotel, everyone was still asleep. He went and got coffee for him and some for everyone else and they started to stir when the aroma of coffee filled the room. They had walked so much Saturday they had blisters on their feet. They all unanimously decided they had seen a lot yesterday, too much actually. They were ready to catch the bus back to the beach and relax. The guys were talking about going back in a couple weeks, but Doug sat silent about a return trip to the city.

This group of guys, Paul, Benny, and James were from the midwest states of Indiana, Iowa, and Ohio. Doug had told them he was from California, but he hadn't mentioned he was actually born in Michigan. He didn't share a lot of his background readily and tended to save that information for only close friends. Last night, Paul told him they all thought Doug was a lot older than them, even though they were the same age. Filling them in on his past wasn't something he wanted to do, so he would remain the cool kid from California.

Twenty-three students started in his signal school class and Paul, Benny and James seemed to be doing well and weren't causing any problems and that was why Doug was hanging out with them. There were a couple guys in the class that Doug would've placed bets on to be the 'least likely to graduate.' While this was unfortunate, it was predictable based on their demeanor and study habits. Before his change of fortune, he was a loser, so he certainly could spot someone who was headed down that same path.

Chapter 38

Graduation and the Jersey Shore

About two weeks before Doug graduated on a Thursday, they were all in their regular orders meeting and he was called up. Doug had heard they might be receiving their orders and he was hoping to go to Europe, but he didn't have much choice in the matter. When he opened his envelope and read, he was going to Metz, France, he was shocked. 'I'm going to Europe on *Uncle Sam's* dime! Yes, please and thank you very much.'

Other guys were going to Europe as well, but not Metz. Finally, he would be able to relax a little and make some long-term friends once he got there. Doug had been saving his money and annual leave so he could have it when he reached his assignment. He wanted to pack up his shit and hit the road at that very moment, but first things first, he had to graduate and take care of other arrangements before leaving. This included getting a lot of vaccinations and making sure all of his documents were in order.

Two weeks later, Dougie was graduating from signal school, with honors! July 5, 1956, indeed, was a proud day for him; it was the first time he graduated from anything related to school. That very same day he got a promotion to private first class, grade E-3. How he wished he had someone to share this moment with, but he rejoiced with his fellow students and went out with them. For their mess meal after graduation, they were treated to a steak dinner. Students who graduated totaled 21, not 23 and they were rewarded with a three-day pass.

For his long weekend, Doug traveled with a couple other graduates who couldn't go to the bars either, due to their ages. One of the grads, Dominick, was familiar with the beaches in New Jersey and he had a car. They all piled in the car, and headed south to Atlantic City, Ocean City and Cape May.

The trip was relaxing, but Atlantic City was crazy. Lots of people were everywhere. He thought it was strange that east coast beach cities had boardwalks, made of wood, but west coast beach cities had concrete sidewalks. Atlantic City gave him the same vibe as New York City—too many fucking people everywhere. They went to the beach for a bit one morning, but when crowds started to gather, around noon, they went walking around and checked out the other sights. They had been warned multiple times if they got too sunburned, they could be disciplined so they either stayed covered up with a long-sleeved shirt or went inside during the heat of the day. After a while they decided to head to Ocean City and then to Cape May, where they spent the night.

By the time he left for Europe, he had saved a little over $200, no thanks to his mom; her cut of his pay was $44 a month. The other $44 was all his and he tried not to spend more than ten bucks a month. All he had to worry about was haircuts and some other basic items. *Uncle Sam* had been footing the bill for everything else he needed. Doug learned that he might leave as early as Thursday. He would catch a prop transport plane from McGuire Air Force Base in New Jersey, refuel in Goose Bay, Labrador, Canada, then refuel in Prestwick Airbase, Airbase in Scotland and in the end land in Frankfurt am Main, Germany and from there he would take a train to Metz.

When Thursday rolled around, he was more than ready to go. Ten guys from signal school were heading to Europe, and while Doug had been on a plane a couple of times, this flight would be the longest of them all, about 20 hours in total, but he was looking forward to the adventure!

Chapter 39

France And the Sights

Doug could sleep anywhere, and this was true for the transport plane. It was a long flight, but he was able to sleep at least half of it, between landings and take-offs. They finally touched down in Frankfurt and were given the option to sleep or catch the next train to their final destination. Doug chose to take the train.

He finally ended up in Metz after eight hours on different trains. Being on the train gave him a chance to get his first glimpse of Europe. There were parts of the train ride where towns seemed unscathed, but there were many areas where the bombing aftermath was still evident. This really brought home how much the war had affected Europe. This was quite a contrast to the United States, where the land was unscathed from World War II, except for Pearl Harbor and a few other incursions on the coasts of the U.S.

When Doug got to Metz, a couple of soldiers met him at the station and gave him a ride to his new home, the U.S. Army Quartermaster Depot in Metz. There he reported for duty and was shown where he was going to be living. The depot was small in relation to the other bases he had been assigned, which was fine with him.

Doug learned he would be on the second floor of the barracks, and he would meet his team the following day to understand what he would be doing going forward. He arranged his stuff in the room that he shared with three others and settled in for the night.

The next day he reported for duty after having breakfast and got briefed on what he would be doing. This assignment was going to be easy. His sergeant told him, "If you can have my radios running and there are no issues with them, you can have a three-day pass every weekend."

Doug thought: 'Hmmm, a three-day pass every weekend when you are stationed in France. It doesn't get any better than this.'

Doug took the first week to familiarize himself with everything and by the end of the second week he had all the equipment up and running without any issues. True to his word, his sarge gave him a 3-day pass. Doug had met quite a few guys who had arrived two-to-three months ahead of him. His coolest new friends, by far, were Phil Albanese and Ron Riker. They were smooth talkers, from the New York City area. They had both come out of college with degrees and were now fulfilling their duties in the military.

Phil was given $1900 by his family to buy a brand-new Mercedes to drive around Europe. After a year, he was supposed to send it to the States. Phil's parents had learned of a tax loophole benefit for purchasing European cars. This involved purchasing and driving the car around Europe for a year, before shipping it home to Long Island. Phil was driving around a brand-new luxury car and Doug made fast friends with him. They used to call Phil 'Cool Breeze' Albanese, because wherever he went women would swoon.

Ron Riker grew up in Greenwich Village in Manhattan and his whole family was musical. They not only played instruments but sang as well. He was heavy into jazz, and he played many instruments, including guitar, saxophone, piano, and trumpet. Every couple weeks, he would perform a one-man show on the stage at the recreation hall. Shortly after they met, he taught Doug how to play the bongos so he could help Ron keep beat when he was playing his instruments.

Doug also hung out with Jim Niemann from California, Roy Phillips from New Mexico, Ken Dingle from Texas, Bob Keyes, from Philly, Joe Coyle from New Jersey, Chuck Wandell from Ohio, and Jack Veneman from Pittsburgh. They were all from different states, which meant a guy could take a cross-country trip and visit each person if so inclined after he got out of the army.

For Doug's first weekend on leave, Phil and Jim invited him to go to Paris, so they left first thing Friday morning, and they were in Paris by noon.

It was hard for Doug to believe less than a year before he had been struggling to survive on his own and yet there he was in Paris. How quickly his fortune had turned. Doug wanted to take advantage of this first visit and see it all. Everywhere he looked were things and places he had only seen in movies or magazines, and he kept pinching himself to make sure it wasn't a dream.

At night, they went to the Moulin Rouge area of Paris. There were nude and topless cabaret shows. The guys teased him it was Dulin Rouge, because if you looked at the sign from just the right angle, with no M and only showing half the O, it did look like it said Dulin Rouge. Within that area of Paris, Doug found things he couldn't find anywhere else in town. Doug was no stranger to women, but the French women were another story—they didn't shave anywhere, which was for some unknown reason sexy to Doug. He loved the way they smelled, it was musky and au naturel. That first night he visited the red-light district and knew he would be back in the future.

Much later that night they soaked in the view of Paris from Sacre Coeur, which was incredible. Sacre Coeur was a brilliantly white stoned Catholic church perched on the tallest butte in the Montmartre area of Paris. Doug and his buddies sat on the top steps and hung out with the large crowd that gathered that night. It was crazy how many people were sitting on the steps in the dark admiring the lights of Paris. One person started singing and the whole rest of the crowd joined in, and it was lovely. Doug didn't know the song, but it was enough to sit and absorb the feeling of being together with a group of people, not French, not English, not American, just people.

As they went back to their hotel, Doug was full of hope for what tomorrow would bring in that magical place.

Phil had been to Paris before and was going to check out some museums. This left Jim and Doug the day to tour the Eiffel Tower, Arc de Triomphe, and the Louvre. Doug was amazed by the Eiffel Tower's structure and was incredulous how this had been built by the same person who created the Statue of Liberty, where he had been a few short months before. Eiffel had built the tower for the World's Fair in 1889 and yet it was still standing, much like Lady Liberty. What an engineer. He thought it was funny that Hitler tried to a display a Nazi flag on the tower but couldn't because the lifts had been disabled. When they were at the top, Doug shouted "Vive la France!" Jim glanced over at Doug and grinned.

Doug wasn't much of an art snob, but he did want to gaze upon the 'Mona Lisa' at the Louvre. When he finally did see her, he was surprised by how small she was, but her smile was just as mysterious as he had seen in books. Up close she was even more enigmatic. Doug took some time checking out the Egyptian section, which was fascinating. The paintings he viewed by Pizarro, Degas, and Renoir were breathtaking. There was something about the way the colors blended and how the light played off the textures and the light-colored paint applied in just the right places. He learned these were Impressionist painters.

Doug was most impressed with the size of the grounds of the palace that housed the Louvre. The statues that surrounded the squares had been important people to France, not just a few, but everywhere you looked they were staring out at you. Doug thought about the sheer effort of building these palaces. It was hard for him to grasp as nothing compared to this in the states. It wasn't like there were any kings or queens to build palaces for, particularly in Detroit.

From the museum, they walked over to Notre Dame and checked out the huge church. As Doug stood and gazed at the cathedral, he paused to reflect that all of this was to worship God. Doug thought it was super cool how the gargoyles on the facade of the cathedral had funny faces and poses. He also liked to imagine how old they were and what they had seen over the years. While he didn't think these beasts were around for the French Revolution, it was a possibility they had been hanging about for Napoleon or the first president of France. They had definitely watched the Eiffel Tower being erected and witnessed Hitler's minions goose-stepping their Nazi asses through the streets of Paris. These monster-people watcher's eyes were always open and if they could talk, he wondered what they would say.

Jim and Doug grabbed a taxi to take them around Paris to take in the sights and Doug was surprised to see an Egyptian obelisk. The driver dropped them off at the Arc de Triomphe to walk around the Avenue des Champs-Élysées. Toward the end of their ambled walk down the avenue, they stopped at a sidewalk bistro to eat.

Doug had oysters, wonderful soup, and bread along with an exquisitely prepared halibut. Jim and Doug took it all in and about three beers later Doug was feeling great. Jim had been around Paris before and could navigate to where they were staying. Just for good measure, they had a couple more beers with Phil in the hotel bar after which Doug passed out for the night.

In the morning, they took their time getting up and eating breakfast, which was another culinary delight for Doug. Although he had eaten croissants before, he had never had anything close to what he had been eating lately. Croissants in Paris melted in his mouth. Doug loved them so much he always ate two of them at a time.

There was no drinking on the way back to Metz until they stopped at a bar next to the base, Café de Frescaty. Doug was impressed with the ambience and friendly staff. This was his friends favorite bar, and they even had a place where they normally sat. They introduced him to Francois and her husband Jean who owned the restaurant and bar. They spoke wonderful English and he felt like this would end up being his home away from home. That was where they camped out until they headed back to base, a little before midnight.

Chapter 40

Settling In

In Doug's barracks up on the third-floor lived two veterans who had been in World War II. Every once in a while, he would get a glimpse of them, but everyone was told to steer clear of them. They were both alcoholics and had seen and been in horrific field and combat situations. The commander in charge of the depot left them alone. Every so often, one of the men would take off AWOL for a few days. Nothing ever happened when they took off. If this had been of the regular GI's, they would have been disciplined. Doug didn't want to know what they had been through, so he left them alone.

Doug and his friends had a weekly routine, which was: one night they would watch a movie, one night drink at Frescaty, one night a week they would go to the enlisted men's club on base for half priced drinks, and one night when they usually stayed in. When they went to Frescaty, they usually made a night of it. Beer was cheap, ten cents a beer and a quarter for a mixed drink. Doug stuck with beer. They stayed at Frescaty until they absolutely had to be back on base, which was midnight. Sometimes the guys, including Doug, would fall asleep in the booths and Francoise would put a blanket on them until it was time to go. Her husband would roust them at about ten minutes to midnight, throw them in his cab and drop them off at the gate.

On any given night if you were in the barracks, you could play a game of craps, which was basically rolling dice in the hall. The barracks were set up to where four soldiers bunked per room, but the layout could be changed into one great room where everyone hung out. The doorways were wider than normal, almost double the size. and when all the doors were open, which was all the time, the space was huge. When a dice game was going, all kinds of people would show up. Those participating included cooks, non-commissioned officers, and of course the guys who were living in the barracks. If you were a newcomer, chances were, you'd get fleeced. Doug had played a lot of street games and was savvy enough to avoid losing money. He never let his guard down.

A poker game occurred at least once a week. He watched several games before he sat down to play. Doing so allowed him to learn the players and watch for tells. Once he thought he had figured out the player's quirks, he would have them deal him in on a hand. Doug liked to play and learn from some of the more seasoned players, so one day he too could be a card shark.

The trick for any of the gambling was to never forget that you were playing with money. The military paid them in script, which was not actual money, but it had denominations on it. Even the coins were paper. Some guys forgot this was their hard-earned pay because the military script seemed more like play money. If you wanted to exchange script for francs, the going rate at the base was 300 francs for every dollar of script.

Doug was lucky to have a sergeant who was cool, but Jack was not. His sergeant made him work Monday through Friday, even though there wasn't a lot of work to do. Jack drove a Jeep from the motor pool off base about five miles to a warehouse in Woippy. At the warehouse it was just Jack and one other GI, making sure all the phone-related equipment stocked in the warehouse made up a complete set, in one box. When someone needed that equipment, it would be ready for use. Jack didn't leave the warehouse for lunch. Since he was off base a truck would come around and sell bread and other baked goods as well as hot dogs.

The sucky part about working at the warehouse was that the French workers got two hours off for lunch and during that time they were allowed to drink wine. Jack didn't have to supervise them, so it didn't affect him too much, but he imagined it was hard to manage the workers in the afternoon. Jack would see some of them staggering around toward the end of the day.

During the day right after work, Doug found time take correspondence school classes in order to obtain his GED certificate. Since he hadn't graduated high school and now had better study habits thanks to the signal school, he wanted to study for and pass the GED test. After this was taken care of, he was going to work on getting college credits.

Doug visited many places during his first six months in France which included Heidelberg, Germany, Luxembourg City, and Paris a couple more times. The favorite place for his crew to visit was Luxembourg. It was a quick train or car ride.

Luxembourg was inviting. It was hard to explain the appeal, but it mainly came down to the people. The citizens were able to speak three to four languages, were more worldly, and the culture was very open.

The first time Ron and Phil took Jack to Luxembourg, they stopped at a bar. It was about eleven in the morning and the second they walked through the door Jack was struck by how full the place was and how everyone was drinking, smoking, and dancing so early in the day.

Jack thought 'I wonder what in the hell is going on?' He picked a corner to sit and watch the room.

Finally, it occurred to him, 'This is a brothel!'

The first thing that clued him in was all the women were very beautiful and super friendly. The other observation Jack made was that after a while, a couple who had been dancing would disappear and then about twenty minutes later come back into the room.

Jack continued to frequent Luxembourg but branched out to other bars and restaurants instead of going to the brothels.

Jack had a girlfriend in Luxembourg, who was coincidentally named Margo. She was pretty and sophisticated. She was German and worked for the French Ambassador to Luxembourg as an au pair for the family's children. She spoke at least four different languages: German, French, English and something called Luxembourgish. The guys would accompany Jack when he went to visit her. They would get up early on Saturdays and either take the train or pile into a car and head over to meet Margo and any girlfriends she brought along. They usually split off to take in the sights around Luxembourg and would meet up later at a restaurant for dinner and then go out to dance and party. They would all head back to Metz on Sunday nights.

On Doug's first trip, he discovered the exchange rate in Luxembourg was much better than the army's rate. You could exchange a dollar (greenback) for 450 francs, which amounted to a little over 33 percent profit over the base exchange rate of 300 francs. He wanted to try something out on one of the trips. He exchanged $100, from his savings to francs. He figured out a system to lend money that worked. He would loan out francs at 350 francs per dollar but insisted that he be paid back in greenbacks. When he was repaid, he would go to Luxembourg and exchange dollars to francs again to keep the pump primed.

The more money he loaned out the more he made. All in all, he was clearing about $20-$100 a month depending on how much he had to loan.

The reason the army used script was to fight local inflation. If the greenbacks were hard for the locals to obtain, it kept their local currency propped up. Sometimes a black market would pop up for buying and selling script. The military fought this by issuing new script to soldiers and provided a conversion day to trade in their old script for the new script. At the end of that day, the old script was no longer valid.

Another sideline business Doug had involved making and selling open-faced egg sandwiches. The army would sponsor dances in town, and he would beat the crowd back to the base by about an hour. Everyone had to be back on base by midnight. On Friday and Saturday nights a lot of drunk soldiers would walk through the main gate.

French bread, eggs, butter, and cheese were the main items Doug needed to cook up his sandwiches for those arriving back on base. These would be open faced and served with a couple napkins. Timing was everything, and Doug timed it so that by the time the GIs started coming in the gate they would smell the butter, bread, cheese, and eggs wafting through the base to the main gate. The revelers were helpless to resist. Doug sold his sandwiches for a dollar and was typically sold out by 1am. On a lucrative night he went through two loaves of bread, a pound of butter, a block of cheese and a couple dozen eggs with his total cost being less than ten cents a sandwich. These weekends he typically made $50 selling sandwiches.

Doug was able to purchase a 1952 Hillman Minx for $125, which he kept at the depot. The vehicle belonged to a GI who was leaving and heading back to the United States. It was a decent car and had bench seats so he could fit four other guys in the car along with him. He would gas it up at the motor pool and each passenger would bring a jerry can of gas, five gallons worth, as well as pay to go on the trip. Depending on where they went, they would also kick in some cash for wear and tear. They took the trains all over, but when they wanted to go somewhere the trains didn't run, they took his car.

Pay-wise Doug was making $90 a month, of which his mother was taking half his pay as his dependent, so every little bit helped, and this allowed Doug to save money for his future. Most months he was netting around $120 to $150 bucks on top of the $45 he received in pay, and after a few months he had quite a bit of working capital. The best thing about these side businesses was that his mom would never see a dime of that money.

Chapter 41

Bar Fights with the French

'Well shit!' Margo had written him a letter. Someone must have told her how to get in touch with him. She talked about what was going on in her life, how she was still working at Skadron. It was a four-page letter, but not one fucking word about taking half his pay. Her new, new, boyfriend and she were still living in San Bernardino. Doug wasted no time in his reply which was on a postcard and was short and sweet. "Stop taking half my army pay now!" That was it, no love Douglas, or any sappy shit, just stop being a mooch.

Doug was so angry after he got the letter, he started a letter writing campaign and sent them to his Aunt Babe, and all his uncles. In his letters he told them what she was doing, hoping they would apply enough pressure on their sneaky sibling to guilt her into stopping the allocation. At least they would know what she was doing.

That weekend Jim and Doug were sitting drinking at their favorite bar, Frescaty, and may have drank a little too much. They thought it might be exciting to go to another bar across the way that happened to be off limits. Thirty to forty percent of the population of France were members of the communist party and the bar was rumored to be a communist bar.

On the way over, Doug started to second guess himself, but by the time he thought about turning around Jim was already in the door. Jim sat down, ordered a beer and shortly after a tiny French men said some shitty thing about the U.S. in French to Jim. Almost immediately, Doug had to join in and defend him. At this time, Jim and Doug were both about 220 pounds and six feet three inches tall, compared to a typical French man who was about 110 -120 pounds and five foot five on a good day.

They had to fight a couple of them, and the rest ran out of the bar, essentially leaving it empty. Doug saw the military policemen were coming so they ran out the back of the bar and headed down the street and then doubled backed to their bar across the street.

About 15 minutes later the military policemen came in to check out the bar. They set their sights on Doug and Jim and stood there behind them for a minute waiting for them to turn around. One of the policemen asked, "Hey, does anybody here know anything about a fight across the street at the commie bar?"

Jim looked at Doug and Doug looked at Jim. Doug, being blessed with the bullshit gene, volunteered, "I didn't see anything, what about you Jim?"

Jim shook his head and said, "No me neither."

"Well, Dulin, can you tell us why your knuckles are all bloody and scraped up?"

"Well, Jim and I were having a good old time and we had to take a piss, so we went outside and while I was standing there, Jim told me I had the smallest dick he has ever seen. I don't know about you, but those are fighting words, so we got into a nasty fight. After we were done, we came back inside, had a beer and patched things up again between us."

One of the policemen said: "Well listen up, if you see those two guys that went over there, I want you to tell them to not go in that bar anymore."

Doug replied, "You got it, we will let them know if we see them."

Doug knew the MPs didn't like the commies any more than they did so that was why there were no consequences, but it would take Doug a while before he got in any more bar fights.

Chapter 42

San Tropez

As the summer of 1957 rolled around, Ron and Doug planned a trip to visit San Tropez. They were able to take a month's leave together. July was supposed to be the most exciting time to be at the French Riviera. Ron had overhead some GIs talking about how much fun it was there. Ron decided he needed to see it for himself. From what he gathered, apparently, there were topless and nude beaches and in general, beautiful, sun-kissed women everywhere. This sounded like the perfect place to relax and pretend they were not in the army.

They were going to drive, and since they would be burning through a lot of gas, they tried to stock up, filling the whole trunk with jerry cans ahead of leaving. Ron had brought all his instruments and had a grandiose idea of being able to find a nightly engagement at one of the clubs, so they wouldn't need to spend their own cash. Doug could play the bongos and that was it, but that's all Ron needed. Ron was so excited at the prospect of a paying gig that he was non-stop chattering.

Ron celebrated his past paying performances. "There is nothing like it. If you are good, and we will be good, you can see it in their faces. The women in particular end up being fans and when they stare at you it is with pure adoration. You can almost see stars sparkling in their eyes."

Hearing him talk about it made Doug eager to experience this feeling as well. The only thing he had experienced from an audience when performing, with Ron, were GIs clapping.

It took about ten hours to make it to San Tropez, as they made several stops along the way to take photos. Their longest stop was in Lyon to eat and buy more gas.

They pulled into St. Tropez at around 7pm. Ron found a place to stay for a few nights and once they had settled in, they hit the town.

They visited all the nightclubs, but Ron had settled on Les Cave. Ron thought he could do a better job than the current act that went on from 2am to 6am. Ron just listened and arranged to meet with the owner the following night.

The next day they slept in, and when they woke up, they went down to the beach for some breakfast, and then Doug fell asleep again for an hour while they were on the beach. Doug didn't understand how he could fall asleep being surrounded by so many beautiful women, but if the body wants sleep, it usually wins.

They went to Les Cave around 10pm when the first group was playing. Doug had never played for cash, only pleasure, so he let Ron do all the talking when it came down to negotiating. Ron chatted with the owner, and they were given an opportunity to play from 2am to 3am as a trial that night. By the early morning hours, they had a paying gig for 50 bucks a night and the owner was going to let them stay on his sailboat in front of the club.

The next day they checked out of the hotel and started staying on the boat. The boat was beautiful. Below the deck was varnished wood, with two berths in the front and two in the main area, which could be converted to a place to sit by adding a table that was stored in the aft of the boat. There was a small galley and a head onboard, but the owner said to use the restroom behind the club. For showers, they would make do with the ocean or one of the showers along the beach. The deck was crowded with skylights and gear, but the cockpit up top was spacious and was another area to entertain people.

The guys didn't need to cook, as they would eat their main meal at the club, free of charge. Doug told Ron, "The only thing I need every day first thing is my coffee with fresh cream and a croissant with eggs."

Ron agreed, "Let's buy a French press for the coffee and beyond that, let's not cook on board. It's less to clean up. We can grab the croissant and eggs at the bakery."

The next night they began the gig, and the owner came over right before they started, he spoke fluent English and said, "You nailed it last night, not only was your sound spot on, but much more professional than the other 2am guys. Ron, you have a gift for getting the crowd involved."

Ron said, "It's in my blood, my family has been playing and performing my whole life, in Greenwich, New York City. I learned from the best."

Doug had known Ron was cool, but securing this job and being able to keep it for the time being was super cool. Ron and Doug took it all in and while they were in St. Tropez, they had a great time. Doug also brushed up on his French and his pickup lines improved greatly. During this time, they each cleared more cash in four days than either of them made in a full month. They split the proceeds 50/50, but Doug thought this was hardly fair as Ron was the talent. Ron insisted on an equal split for the gigs.

Having the sailboat to stay on was amazing. It was moored a couple hundred feet in front of the club. Girls from everywhere stayed in St. Tropez. Ron and Doug invited quite a few friendly visitors to come aboard the boat in the afternoons before their shows, and sometimes they would be followed back from the club due to their charming banter and flirting.

They would also meet various movie stars in the club. One thing Doug noted was that 'the beautiful people' weren't always as beautiful up close or when they spoke. There were plenty of gorgeous women and men hanging out all the time at Les Cave.

One of Doug's favorite pastimes, other than being with girls, was sitting in a bistro and people watching… and there was plenty to watch. There was a beach where sunbathing topless was legal, and when women were clothed, they pushed the limits of decency with no bras and short shorts, things one would never see stateside.

Men would walk around shirtless and had these short shorts that looked like they were wearing some type of underwear, but super tight. They would strut around showing off their physiques like peacocks. Some had a right to be proud, but others had no business wearing those kind of bathing suits. Doug was sticking with his regular swim shorts—although he felt like he could strut with the best of them.

Ron and Doug got two nights off a week from the club, Mondays, and Tuesdays. They decided to rent a motorcycle and ride from St. Tropez to La Spezia which was a beautiful city on the coast of Italy. Buildings in the town were painted different colors and were spectacular. Ron rented a scooter when they got there to tour the city. Although they didn't understand Italian, they were able to make their way around town. That night they ate at a trattoria ordered food and a bottle of Chianti. As they sat and absorbed the scenery, both agreed they had lucked out being able to stay and play in San Tropez.

They performed the rest of their shows and arranged to leave two days before they had to report back. The Les Cave owner wanted Ron and Doug to stay on and take over for the opening act, as they drew a larger crowd than them. Ron had to explain a couple of times that they were in the army and really needed to get back on base or they would be arrested. The owner finally relented, and they headed back to Metz. The whole way back they reminisced about the trip and how much fun they had. They rolled into base, flush with cash, almost four hundred bucks a piece. A couple of fat cats, with a great musician's story.

Chapter 43

Amsterdam

The first time Doug went to Amsterdam he did quite a bit of window shopping in the red-light district, however the novelty wore thin quickly, and he found other things to occupy his time. There was a six-month period where he would spend every other weekend visiting the city. The laid-back atmosphere, the canals, and the general free thinking of the Dutch really appealed to him.

One of his favorite places to go was the Rijksmuseum. Doug mainly went to look at "The Night Watch" by Rembrandt. This painting was huge, about 12ft high and over 14ft wide. He liked to sit in front of it and take it all in. After a while of contemplating the painting, many things began to appear in the shadows just past the three main characters. Other Rembrandts and a couple Van Gogh paintings were displayed there as well as many other famous paintings.

Looking at art created hundreds of years ago had Doug thinking about the creators of these works. Their art and ideas had survived. The artists was able to reach up through the centuries and share a moment of intimacy with him. He was struck with the knowledge that life is fleeting and way too short to settle on a boring existence. He thought, 'If the great Dutch Masters couldn't figure out how to slow down the passage of time, what made him think he could do anything to stretch it out? Mortality is a motherfucker.'

Doug really liked Amsterdam, especially when he spent time with Ilse. She was a lovely girl who had fallen on hard times and was doing whatever she could to survive. He first met her when he was sitting in the Dam square, and they hit it off. When Doug came to town, he would take her out on a canal cruise, go for a bike ride, or visit different areas of the city.

After spending a few different weekends with her, she took him up to her very small room, which was similar to what he had at the gas station. Ilse worked two jobs, and her family wasn't around. She didn't go into detail about her background and Doug didn't ask. This was something they had in common as neither of them talked about their past. It wasn't a super serious relationship, but they both enjoyed the time they spent together, and he would help her out when she needed cash.

Ilse took him to Rotterdam and Haarlem. Rotterdam was not an incredibly interesting city as it appeared to be like a lot of cities back home, especially in the west. The coolest thing about the town was the port. Doug learned that the main part of Rotterdam got bombed and burnt out in one attack known as the 'Rotterdam Blitz' in World War II. That explained why it was all brand new. People in the Netherlands thought Rotterdam showcased a well-planned city, but compared to the rest of Europe, Doug found it to be cold and sterile.

Haarlem was a different story; Doug was impressed with Grote Market square and how lively it was on the weekend he was there. At the market, many things were available such as herring preserved in salt with onions, tulip bulbs and flowers, and many other items from Dutch culture. Doug wasn't a fan of the herring, but he ate one at Ilse's urging.

The area around the square was anchored by a huge old church, called, the Grote Kerk or St. Bavokerk, which housed a huge organ. Doug overheard a tour guide say that Handel and a young Mozart, as well as many other composers, traveled to play the organ, which at one time was the largest in the world.

One thing he observed about the Dutch was that they didn't go to church much, but there were a lot of churches in the country, one or two for every town square. Doug thought this may be the case for quite a few of the countries that had been affected by World War II. If the war was fought on the ground, or families were torn apart forever, the people lost their belief in a god. The Netherlands was no exception to this, but they showed their contempt more outwardly by not going to church and not taking care of the church structures. In some towns, the churches were completely re-purposed for other uses. The Grote Kerk was locked the day he visited Haarlem and that was a shame.

The ride out to the Keukenhof gardens was beautiful. Doug wasn't particularly interested in flowers, but the fields were very colorful and breathtaking. Ilse told Doug, "The tulip is very important to the Dutch economy. Not only do we export a lot of tulip bulbs, but we also grow many other bulbs such as daffodils. We have to plant the bulbs, so they multiply and then we split them apart, once the bloom cycle is over, we replant the 'babies' from the original bulb again or sell them to overseas buyers."

Doug asked, "How do you know so much about bulbs?"

"It is something you are aware of from a young age. It's part of the culture."

As soon as they walked through the gates and into the gardens, Doug said, "Wow, breathtaking!"

Ilse was happy to show him around and name each of the different types of flowers like the crocus, hyacinths, and different sizes of daffodils. The focal feature of the landscape was a large pond with different plantings of tulips all along the edges of it and large white swans swimming on the serene water. They took a leisurely stroll through the garden where they found a bench to sit and cuddle a little, Doug even sneaked in a kiss.

They spent about two hours in the garden and made their way back to Amsterdam. Doug had a room at a local hotel where he and Ilse spent the night after a delicious dinner. The next day Ilse had to work so he was on his own. Doug left and went to Amsterdam Central Station to catch his train.

Doug really liked the Amsterdam station, which was one of the larger train stations he'd been to. It was gothic, but also looked like an intricate gingerbread house. The station was very similar in architecture to the Rijksmuseum and that's because the same architect, Pierre Cuypers, built both structures. Both buildings were a combination of red and whitish bricks in various shades and designs. There were two huge clock towers built into the outside of the train station structure that were facing toward the center of town, the back of the station was facing the waterfront.

When you walked inside the station it was cavernous, the main entry was wide open. Holding up the grand roof were huge columns along the perimeter. It was a building to behold. The columns were so thick that ten people could easily stand behind one of them and no one would be able to see them.

This large area was a perfect place to people watch. Doug stood in the corner and watched people coming out of the various areas of the station. When travelers got to this area, they paused, looked around lost and either approached someone who seemed official to ask questions, or continued to wander outside.

That time when he was at the station, he was watching a small family group who came out of the tunnels. As they were walking the older man who had a cane, slowed his pace, and then hid behind one of the large columns. The middle-aged man and woman walked outside. As soon as they were gone, the old man hightailed it out another exit. The pair came back indoors and were scrambling around desperately searching for the man with the cane. Doug edged closer and pretended to examine a piece of paper and could hear they were siblings who had just 'lost' their dad. It was comical to him, but they sure were in a snit about it. The sly old man had pulled one over on them. Still chuckling, Doug went to catch his train.

Chapter 44

Brussels World's Fair 1958

In July of 1958, Doug, Ron, Phil, Jack, and Jim went to the Brussels World's Fair. The trip took about four hours, and they planned on spending at least three days in Brussels. Many people traveled from all over the world to visit and the crowds were huge. Everyone was dressed up for the event and Doug and his buddies were no exception. They were looking sharp wearing their suits and ties.

When they first arrived and entered the grounds, Jack said, "I have never seen a landscape quite like this, it's really spectacular." The flower beds and grass were breathtaking and perfectly planted with different patterns of flowers for each area.

Doug's first impression was that everything was modern. Jim really liked the United States building, which had a water feature outside. He marveled, "I count over 25 American flags here, it's fantastic to see something from home."

The building was built to show a movie called *America The Beautiful*, which was put together by The Walt Disney

Company. The movie was shown in a round building with all the screens surrounding the audience who were standing in the center of the building. During the showing, Doug and his friends were amazed at what they were watching and afterwards, Phil said, "It felt like we were flying, let's go again." It was called a 'Circarama' and was a complete 360-degree show with eleven cameras. Doug liked this so much he watched it three times. Each time he came out, he grabbed ice cream and a Coke at the Pavilion and went back and waited in line.

There were other buildings that featured American life and it was cool to go through them and see things from all over the U.S. The layout and displays seemed to say: "It's fun here, you should visit!"

Across the way was the U.S.S.R. building. The contrast between the U.S. and the U.S.S.R. buildings was dramatic. For one, the United States building was round, and the Soviet building was rectangular. When the guys walked in, they were struck by the statues, the largest being of Lenin himself.

Jim said, "It's like they are still worshipping a leader, one man, instead of embracing democracy. They are trying too hard to show they are superior, but it falls flat for me. This looks like an old man's ideas for the future."

Doug did think they were trying too hard. The only thing, technology-wise, that was cool was the model of Sputnik, but right next to that were rockets which was in-your-face aggression. The exhibits seemed as if they were still stuck in the last two decades. Even the cars they had on display were super boxy and clunky compared to the newest sleeker models of cars in the states.

The U.S. showed a movie that demonstrated technology and the beauty of the states, while this building was focusing on agricultural and machinery as if they were pumping their chest out and saying, "Hey, it's not that bad over here."

Doug couldn't quite put his finger on it, but something gave him an uneasy feeling while he was in the building. He was fairly confident everyone who went into the building was being recorded for sound and film. The building was stark and militaristic. As Doug walked out, he physically tried to shake off the weird feeling he had.

Doug was keenly interested in civil engineering, forestry, and seeing the planetarium, but he also wanted to go to the different countries' buildings. Many of the other countries were still struggling with rebuilding after the war and it showed in their displays, as they were not showy, were rather smaller, and low on the wow factor. All of the buildings were very angular had a space-age feel with the exception of a few buildings such as Thailand and Morocco.

A cable tram system ran from one end of the main avenue to the other end past the Atomium, which was a giant model of a cell with each sphere representing an atom. The Atomium was definitely the center piece of the fair and spectacular to behold. It was covered in sheets of aluminum that were polished like a mirror; the effect was stunning. Doug wasn't an engineer, but he had an immense respect for the person who designed this and for the people who built it. The elevator that took visitors to the top of the structure was super-fast and the view from there was worth the wait in the long line to gain entry. It provided a 360-degree view of the World's Fair grounds.

Another unique exhibit was called the Philips Pavilion. Disney's building had everything to do with visual stimulation and the pavilion was an immersive experience of sound. It was an odd structure, composed of curvatures and angles that made the sound resonate throughout the interior.

The sound inside could only be described as perplexing. It was as if hundreds of glass shards were hitting a metal surface or like sparks from a fire; Doug couldn't quite decide which of these it was. Toward the end of the recording, it sounded like glass chains were rattling together or a blacksmith was hammering out a horseshoe, 'tink, tink, tink.' It was definitely something to hear, especially with over 400 speakers playing the recording.

Quite a few of the buildings represented large corporations such as the Kodak and Pan Am Airway Pavilions. The second day they were at the fair, they stayed late. An impressive light show was held at night. All lights flickered and danced, which included the five-point stars around the grounds, the cable car poles lights and the lights on the Ferris wheel. The fountains lights also glowed and flashed in the water. None of the guys had seen a light display like this anywhere.

The next day they went walking around Brussels. The main attraction there was the Manneken Pis which was a tiny statue of a little naked boy peeing in a fountain. Doug didn't understand what the fuss was all about. The locals would dress up the boy in various outfits depending on what was happening in Brussels at the time. Everyone had a joke about it. Ron asked the statue pointing to the fountain, "Is this the urinal? Because I have to pee!"

They toured the Grand Palace and then hit the bar at their hotel. Doug was sitting in the corner when he spied a small chalkboard on the wall. The barkeep gave him some chalk and he started putting hash marks on it for each beer he drank. He was up to about eight. The next thing he remembered was someone shaking him awake. Jim told him it was time to head up to the room.

When Doug looked at the board the next morning, he noticed his last hashmark went all the way down to the ground. He thought, 'That must have been my last beer.' He was amused knowing he had left his mark on Brussels.

Chapter 45

Leaving Metz

As the summer turned to fall, many of Doug's friends had begun to leave and go back to the States. Jack was the first to go.

Jack said, "Doug, isn't it funny how you dread going into the military and all you can think about is going home? Then everything changes when you're sent to Europe. After a while, you don't want to go home, it's been so welcoming over here. Now, I am less interested in going home. I hope you do well. I know you've had a hard time and I just hope it all works out for you."

Toward the end of September, Doug received his orders. In about two weeks' time he would be back in California and would be a civilian again. There were quite a few things to do before he left. He'd already transferred his test scores certifying he had passed his GED to San Bernardino Valley College, but he also needed to make sure his college credits were transferred as well. Doug had two years of college finished at this point and was well on his way to making his goal of getting his bachelor's degree.

Doug had a piece of paper where he was writing everyone's addresses and phone numbers for future contact. He had made some wonderful friends in the army, and he hoped to stay in touch with them over the years. Doug and Jim were the last ones to leave as they had originally arrived within two weeks of each other. Jim had just left to go back to Northern California with his new bride, Josette. She was a really sweet French girl and Jim was incredibly lucky to have her.

Leaving was bittersweet, but Doug didn't want to re-enlist. In his heart, he sensed it was time for this part of his life to wind down. There would be other adventures for him in the future, but he wasn't sure on that day if they would top his time in Europe.

Doug took a couple of days to travel and wrapped things up with his 'girlfriends' and he made a special point to go visit Francoise and Jean.

They were thankful for the gift basket he brought with sheets and nylons for Francoise and American spirits and two cartons of cigarettes for Jean, all items that were hard to come by in France, even in 1958.

Francoise was extremely sweet and sometimes sassy, and she spoke perfect English. She and Doug liked to banter back and forth, and this day was no exception.

Doug said, "I will be back to come and see you. You and Jean have been very kind to me and made all of us feel at home and welcome."

Francoise said, "Aww, you guys always say you'll come back, and no one ever does."

Doug, who was considerably taller than her, stooped down and gazed into her eyes and told her, "I'll come back, you wait and see."

He hugged Francoise and her husband and had to leave before they could see he had tears in his eyes.

The next couple days were a whirlwind. Doug gave away most of his stuff, except his best clothes and a few trinkets he had saved. Chuck agreed to store his stuff till he got back to California, so he shipped important items to him a couple weeks ahead of his departure.

When someone left the depot and was headed home, it ended up being a free-for-all and sometimes a bidding war for the items they didn't take with them. GIs left all kinds of stuff, such as bicycles, radios, clocks, suitcases, bags, coats; you name it, they left it. After a while, unwanted items that were left in the barracks made it to the lost and found. If nobody wanted them after a month, then they were donated to the local church or charities.

Doug was able to sell his car to Jean's cousin for the equivalent of $150, which was higher than what he paid for it. None of the enlisted men could buy it, though, because after Doug purchased his car, enlisted men weren't allowed to have vehicles at depot. He was the last one to have this privilege.

More importantly, Doug would be traveling with considerable cash, and he took precautions for safekeeping it. He was leaving Europe with over $4,000. All along he had been exchanging his $20 bills into $100 bills for easy transport back to the states. Having this money would set him up for success when he arrived home.

As he was leaving, he took one last walk around the depot, said his final goodbyes, and was on his way back to the U.S.

Chapter 46

Homeward Bound

Doug was finally done with all of his paperwork, the physical, and he had received his final pay. It required about three days to muster out of the army, but he was free to catch a bus to Colton. He had decided to make San Bernardino his home.

As Doug walked out of the Greyhound station and was waiting for his buddy Kenny to pick him up, he took a moment to reflect on these past four years. From being told he had the highest IQ the school psychologist ever tested, to enlisting in the army to avoid being arrested, his whole life had changed like a light being turned on or someone snapping their fingers.

He had barely turned 20, had two years of college under his belt, and was armed with the GI bill which meant *Uncle Sam* would pay for him to obtain his bachelor's degree. Standing there assessing his life's progress, Doug was proud of his successes. He was a self-made man headed toward a bright future.

Look out everyone, Dougie's back in town!

Epilogue

Little did Doug know, standing there in October of 1958, what was in store. I know, within two years and a couple months, he would marry and later become a doting father to five children. He would secure a job working for the California Division of Highways, now Caltrans. There he had a successful career, where he supervised the construction of almost 70 bridges in Southern California. In 1978, he would retire from the Caltrans Bridge Department and start a new career selling real estate and establish his own company with several branch offices. During this time, he became an avid boater, pilot, and eventually retired to Lake Havasu. There he remained adventurous by traveling and made many more 'friends for life.' He did go back to Metz to see Francoise, just like he promised. Along the way he had trials and brushes with death, but he was never afraid to make changes if he was unhappy. Come along with me in these next chapters, where I go into detail about those times, which were truly remarkable for a boy with his early childhood background.

Acknowledgments

I am eternally grateful for everyone who helped me while writing this book which includes my friends and family.

My husband, Steve, was great and supported me by playing his guitar upstairs, while I worked downstairs. During this time, he also nursed me back to health while I was double casted for four months (that's another story). I would marry him again. My son, Dulin, who spent time reading my daily writing and offered his twenty-year-old perspective which was invaluable.

I'd also like to thank my first readers who assisted me with advice and questions that greatly contributed to this novel. I am everlasting beholden to Liz and Patti Adams, Dene´ Crandall, Dan Dulin, Craig Hensley, Theresa Lee, Yamel Monjaraz, Guy Palos, Karen Raines, and Jerry Tilley.

I have read this book at least 100 times looking for errors, omissions, and typos, along with two other hired editors. There are probably more errors (I hope not), but I would like to thank Steve Lech for finding additional mistakes including my penchant for run-on sentences, much like this one.

Terri Dulin, my sister-in-law, was my final first reader. I thought I had caught all the typos and was ready to print, however, she found a few more. Thank you, Terri!

I would also like to thank those that helped me when I got stuck and provided valuable information about the army, Jack Veneman, the high school environment, Doug and Barbara Blum and the North End of San Bernardino, Rondy French.

Most of all, I would like to thank my dad for sitting down and going over his life in great detail and my Great-Uncle Chuck for allowing me to interview and record his memories.

Stay in touch at www.dawndickerson.com, and sign up for my newsletter, info@dawndickerson.com, where I send you updates on upcoming books and projects.

-Dawn

Made in the USA
Las Vegas, NV
03 September 2023

77007645R00140